GLOBETROTTER™

Travel Guide

CYPRUS

PAUL HARCOURT DAVIES

NEW
HOLLAND

D0488494

NEW
HOLLAND

★★★ Highly recommended
★★ Recommended
★ See if you can

Fifth edition published in 2007
by New Holland Publishers (UK) Ltd
London • Cape Town • Sydney • Auckland

10 9 8 7 6 5 4 3 2
www.newhollandpublishers.co.za

Garfield House, 86 Edgware Road,
London W2 2EA, United Kingdom

80 McKenzie Street, Cape Town,
8001, South Africa

Unit 1, 66 Gibbes Street, Chatswood,
NSW 2067, Australia

218 Lake Road, Northcote,
Auckland, New Zealand

Distributed in the USA by
The Globe Pequot Press, Connecticut

Keep us Current
Information in travel guides is apt to change, which is
why we regularly update our guides. We'd be grateful
to receive feedback if you've noted something we
should include in our updates. If you have new
information, please share it with us by writing to the
Publishing Manager, Globetrotter, at the office nearest
to you (addresses on this page). The most significant
contribution to each new edition will receive a free
copy of the updated guide.

Publishing Manager: Thea Grobbelaar
DTP Cartographic Manager: Genené Hart
Editors: Nicky Steenkamp, Melany McCallum,
Mary Duncan, Beverley Jollands
Cartographers: Marisa Roman, Nicole Bannister,
Tanja Spinola, Elaine Fick
Design and DTP: Nicole Bannister, Gillian Black
Consultant Updater: Robin McKelvie
Reproduction by Hirt & Carter (Pty) Ltd, Cape Town.
Printed and bound by Times Offset (M) Sdn. Bhd., Malaysia.

Acknowledgements:
The author and publishers thank the following for their
generous assistance during the compilation of this book:
Cyprus Tourist Organization (London and Lefkosia); Lefkos
Christodoulou at the Rodon Hotel; Jenne Davies; Andreas
Demetropoulos of the Cyprus Wildlife Society; Simon
Demetropoulos; Philippos Drousiotis of the Drousia
Heights Hotel; Noel Josephides of Sunvil Holidays;
Sophocles and Diana Markides; Clive and Di Rainbow.

Photographic Credits:
Brian Davis, pages 19, 32; **Jeff Goodman**, page 60; **Paul
Harcourt Davies**, title page, pages 7, 8, 9, 10, 11, 14
(top and bottom), 17 (top), 20, 30, 35, 37, 38, 39, 40,
42, 44, 45, 46, 48 (bottom), 52, 58, 59, 62, 63, 64, 65,
68, 72, 78, 84, 88, 94, 96 (top and bottom), 97, 98, 99;
Robert Harding, pages 106, 108, 114; **G.A. Hill**, pages
85, 112; **Roger G. Howard**, page 23; **Robin McKelvie**,
pages 18, 56; **Stuart Morris**, page 15; **Andreas Nicola**,
pages 4, 21, 22, 24, 25, 26, 27, 36, 48 (top), 54, 70, 73,
74, 75, 76, 77, 86, 87, 91, 100; **Clive Rainbow**, pages
104, 109, 110, 111, 113, 115, 117, 118, 119 (top and
bottom); **Simon Reddy**, page 33; **Brian Richards**, pages
6, 17 (bottom), 28, 29, 34, 41, 47, 57, 101; **Bill
Robinson**, pages 82, 89; **Norman Rout**, page 61;
Schmid Reinhard/Sime/Photo Access, cover; **C. Smale**,
pages 12, 79.

Although every effort has been made to ensure that
this guide is up to date and current at time of going
to print, the Publisher accepts no responsibility or
liability for any loss, injury or inconvenience incurred
by readers or travellers using this guide.

Cover: *Historical ruins of the church at Pafos.*
Title Page: *Ruins of Saranda Colones, Pafos.*

CONTENTS

1
Introducing
Cyprus

Cyprus, **Aphrodite's Isle**, strategically located at the
eastern end of the Mediterranean, has been a prize
long fought over by its numerous conquerors, from the
Phoenicians to the **Greeks**, the **Romans** and the **Turks**
of the **Ottoman Empire**. Its turbulent history, and the
rich and varied cultures of those who have ruled it over
the centuries, have left their mark everywhere. The
island is a huge **archaeological site**, in which treasures
still lie waiting to be discovered.

To the holiday-maker Cyprus promises guaranteed **sunshine** and a vast range of accommodation priced to suit all
pockets, from corporate conferences to backpackers. It
also offers a wealth of interest for those who have had
enough of sitting on the beach. At the height of summer it
may be too hot and crowded for some tastes, but in spring
and early summer a different Cyprus beckons: an island
which, increasingly, is attracting people who enjoy **natural
history** and **walking**. The dry, baked landscape becomes
an oasis of greenery for a while in spring when the land is
dotted with wild **flowers** – anemones, poppies and orchids
– and enlivened by migrating **birds**.

The friendliness and **hospitality** of Cypriots in both
north and south is almost legendary, particularly when
the island is less crowded with tourists, and **children**
are always made very welcome everywhere.

Although the island is still divided following the
Turkish invasion of 1974 this does not have a major
impact on holiday-makers. Cyprus is now also a member
of the European Union.

(Map showing TURKEY, CYPRUS with Lefkosia (Nicosia), Larnaka, Pafos, Lemesos (Limassol), and MEDITERRANEAN SEA)

Opposite: *The Roman temple
of Apollo Hylates, Kourion,
one of a rich collection of
archaeological sites in Cyprus.*

THE LAND

After Sicily and Sardinia, Cyprus is the third largest island in the Mediterranean. It falls into four major topographical regions: the forested **High Troödos**, the arid **Troödos foothills** along the southern flanks, the plain of the **Mesaoria** and the **Keryneia Mountains** in the north.

Cyprus boasts some 768km (480 miles) of **coastline**, ranging from rocks to long sandy beaches. The sand type varies: dark where the volcanic Troödos descends to the sea, golden or white from the low-lying limestone in the east. The land drops steeply along the south coast, forming spectacular white cliffs with beaches at their feet. Near Lemesos and Famagusta the sea floor shelves, forming deep natural harbours. The Troödos region is an effective cloud trap for the prevailing, mainly westerly, winds, and the important seasonal **rivers** of Cyprus begin here, most now dammed to make year-round use of the water. Deep valleys and gorges show the sculpting effect of the winter streams over the millennia. **Chionistra** (Mount Olympus) is snow-covered from January to March.

Climate

The island's two mountain ranges influence the climate and the high level of sunshine creates considerable temperature differences (both seasonal and day to night) between land and sea. Western coastal areas tend to have slightly cooler summers and somewhat milder winters than the interior.

The climate is classed as 'arid Mediterranean', though there is more seasonal variety than this suggests. Hot and dry summers from June to September and variable winters from November until February/March are separated by a short spring and autumn. Choose spring for flowers, walk in spring and autumn, sizzle on the beach in summer and ski in Troödos in winter.

COMPARATIVE CLIMATE CHART	NICOSIA				PAFOS				LARNAKA			
	WIN JAN	SPR APR	SUM JULY	AUT OCT	WIN JAN	SPR APR	SUM JULY	AUT OCT	WIN JAN	SPR APR	SUM JULY	AUT OCT
MAX TEMP. °C	22	36	40	28	22	30	33	26	21	32	36	27
MIN TEMP. °C	1.3	10	17	6	5	12	19	10	3	12	19	8
MAX TEMP. °F	71	96	103	82	71	86	91	79	70	90	97	80
MIN TEMP. °F	34	50	63	42	41	54	65	50	38	53	65	47
HOURS OF SUN	11	14	13	11	11	14	13	11	11	14	13	11
RAINFALL in	2	–	–	1	3	–	–	2	3	–	–	2
RAINFALL mm	43	–	–	33	80	–	–	55	80	–	–	55

Left: *The Karyotis near Kakopetria becomes a torrent when swollen by melting snow from the Troödos.* **Opposite:** *Summer temperatures close to 38°C (100°F) are the norm, with guaranteed all-day sunshine.*

Geology

The geology of Cyprus has been very closely studied for the clues it gives in support of the **tectonic theory**, which treats the earth's crust as a series of gigantic moving and overlapping plates. Some 19 million years ago the rocks of the Troödos lay beneath the Sea of Tithys. Remains of countless marine organisms deposited on the ocean floor became the chalks and limestones now found on the lower parts of the Troödos. As the earth strained and groaned under forces of unimaginable strength, plutonic rocks, rich in minerals, were forced upwards and the Troödos slowly emerged from deep below the sea. Violent **volcanic eruptions** created the Troödos foothills: molten rocks cooling quickly in the ocean formed the 'pillow lava' seen on the hillsides.

The northern range grew up from the sea floor as movements took place in the northern continental plates. Its limestone dates from a succession of geological periods: Carboniferous at Kantara, Triassic at Dikomo, Jurassic at St Hilarion and Cretaceous at Lapithos.

Until the Pleistocene period, around one million years ago, the **Troödos Massif** and the **Keryneia Mountains** were separate islands. The channel between them gradually silted up to form the **Mesaoria** (which means 'between mountains'): wherever rivers cut through the plain, fossil shells are exposed in the muddy gorges.

A LATTER-DAY
DINOSAUR

The largest lizard in Cyprus, the **starred agama** (*Agama stelio*), grows up to 30cm (12in) long and can be spotted racing up olive and carob trees to hide in crevices in their trunks. At close quarters the agama's head gives the impression of being millions of years old – a memory of the dinosaurs. Greek Cypriots call it the 'nose-biter'; Armenian Cypriots have a less polite name, identifying it as a hazard to inattentive males!

Wildlife

Mammals: In Pleistocene times Cyprus was home to the pygmy elephant, pygmy hippopotamus, ibex, genet and wild boar. The largest mammal is the **mouflon** (*Ovis musimon*). **Foxes** occur in Akamas and Cyprus **hares** (*Lepus cyprius*) survive in small populations between successive hunting seasons. The island has its own races of **shrew** and **spiny mouse**. Eight bat species are recorded: the **fruit-eating bat** (*Rousettus aegyptiacus*) is the most spectacular.

Birds: For the birdwatcher the best times to visit Cyprus coincide with the spring and autumn migrations, though these are never easy to predict. In spring there are vividly coloured **hoopoes**, **rollers** and **bee-eaters** as well as a host of small warblers, of which the best known is the resident **Cyprus warbler**. **Flamingos** feed on the salt lakes, and other water birds include **herons**, **bitterns** and **egrets**. In spring, **demoiselle cranes** include Cyprus in their flight path as they migrate to Asia Minor; in autumn **common cranes** fly over in the opposite direction. Several unique races of birds – **scops owl**, **pied wheatear**, **coal tit**, **jay**, **crossbill** and **short-toed treecreeper** – live in the Troödos.

In Akamas, on the cliffs at Episkopi and in the heights of the Keryneia range look for the **lammergeier** (bearded vulture). Safe within the airbase at Akrotiri, the **Eleonora's falcons** raise their broods to catch the autumn migration. The heights around Kantara are home to **alpine swift**, **blue rock thrush** and **spectacled warbler**.

Right: *The two-tailed pasha (Charaxes jasius) can be spotted on strawberry trees (Arbutus) on the south coast.*

HEDGEHOGS

The **long-eared hedgehog** has had an unhappy time in Cyprus since local superstition gave it a reputation for clambering into chicken coops, intent on having its spiny way with the hens. Physical improbability did not deter the population in their persecution of the innocent creature.

Reptiles and Amphibians: Cypriots harbour a detestation of reptiles out of all proportion to the danger they pose. The **blunt-nose viper** is the only snake on the island poisonous to humans: it has a distinctive yellow, horn-like tail.

Lizards are seemingly everywhere: pale **geckos** emerge on city house walls at night to feed on insects attracted by lights. Tiny green **tree frogs** (*Hyla arborea*), capable of making a noise way out of proportion to their tiny size, can be heard at night in the trees. The most famous of the cold-blooded creatures in Cyprus are the turtles: both **loggerhead** (*Caretta caretta*) and **green turtles** (*Chelonia mydas*) breed on the west coast (*see p. 46*).

Marine Life: The lack of tidal movement around the island, coupled with very few streams providing nutrients to enrich the coastal water, has kept plankton levels and consequently **fish** numbers on the low side. But there is still plenty beneath the waves to intrigue anyone with a snorkel and mask: some 200 species of fish have been documented in the sea around Cyprus.

Insects: Butterflies are the most obviously attractive of the island's insects: large swallowtails are common and visitors may glimpse fast-flying **two-tailed pashas** near strawberry trees. There are many endemic butterflies like the tiny Pafos blue and the yellow Cyprus festoon. Other spectacular insects include several kinds of **praying mantids** and **hawkmoths**.

Right: *Tree frogs (*Hyla arborea*) announce their presence loudly on hot summer nights.*

INSECT PESTS

Locusts migrating from North Africa are no longer the ravaging pests they once were. Early records of the British administration recount that everyone had to kill their quota of locusts and bring them to be weighed: failure meant fines or imprisonment.

In the early days of British occupation many young soldiers died from malaria. Later, swamps were filled and eucalyptus trees planted to drain wet areas. These days, local **mosquitoes** are not malarial but their infernal high-pitched whine can be maddening and some people are allergic to their bites. They are particularly vicious near the salt lakes, but they can be kept at bay indoors using small plug-in vaporizers.

Cyprus vegetation falls into three broad categories. The *phrygana* (**garigue**) is found in lowlands up to 500m (1650ft) and is characterized by low-growing, drought-resistant shrubs (thyme, spiny burnet and cistus) and an abundance of flowering bulbs, herbs and annuals growing in spring in open spaces or sheltered beneath the spiny bushes.

The **maquis** is a zone of taller shrubs and small trees 1–5m (3–16ft) tall, including brooms, terebinth and mastic. It extends up to the **forest zone** and sometimes merges with it as undergrowth. Above 1000–1200m (3300–4000ft) much of the land is forested with conifers.

Other minor plant communities, each with their special plants, include salt marshes, dunes, mountain streams and stone walls.

Many orchid enthusiasts visit Cyprus in spring, finding here a unique assemblage of species which could otherwise only be found by making several journeys much further afield. These include bee orchids, three of which are endemic: **Kotschyi's ophrys**, the **Lapithos ophrys** and the **elegant ophrys**. Later in the year, the Troödos has its own **Troödos helleborine** and, in a few wet places, the rare **eastern marsh helleborine**.

Plant Life

Cyprus' location has made it a veritable collecting basket for plants from Asia Minor, North Africa and the other areas around the Mediterranean. The island's varied flora includes some 1800 species of flowering plants, amongst them over 120 endemic species, including several **orchids**. In spring there is a riot of colourful **shrubs**, **annuals** (such as poppies and crown daisies) and **bulbs**, including narcissus, crocus and tulips. But by the time most visitors arrive in summer the lowland landscape has changed to a parched series of greys and browns – only resilient plants such as thistles are in flower. At the height of summer the white flowers of the sea daffodil (Famagusta lily) appear on sandy beaches.

In the mountains the flowers appear later, beginning with tiny lilac crocus as the snow melts. In May the hillsides are ablaze with bushes of pink and white rock roses and the smell of French lavender hangs in the air.

The open **forests** on the heights of Troödos, above 1200m (4000ft), consist mainly of **black pine**, ancient **juniper** and planted **Cyprus cedar**. On walks, look out for gnarled trees twisted and split by lightning strikes, where the sap within boiled instantly and explosively. At lower altitudes the woods are denser, mainly of Calabrian pine with an under-storey of the Cyprus golden oak (*Quercus alniifolia*) and red-barked eastern strawberry tree (*Arbutus andrachne*). Oak forests (*Quercus veneris*), once widespread, are now only found as occasional trees in the lowlands.

Conservation

There is a growing interest in conservation in the south, particularly amongst the young. That this exists is due to a dedicated band of Cypriots and resident foreigners together with conservation-minded officials in the government departments of Fisheries and Forestry. Exhibitions, lectures and especially television series have increased public awareness. **Hunting** is a national pastime and its impact on migrating birds has been devastating: too often anti-hunting laws are repealed as a matter of political expediency near election time. Bird-liming, although now outlawed, has declined rather than disappeared (*see p. 91*). As prosperity increases more Cypriots are becoming aware of the importance of their diminishing untouched natural heritage and how quickly its time is running out.

If conservation is in its infancy in the south it is in the foetal stage in the north: there is a strong interest in birds through the North Cyprus Society for the Protection of Birds and a museum at Halevga (Alevkaya) dedicated to the rich flora of the north. A tremendous problem in both south and north is **over-grazing** by goats: the arrival of Anatolian settlers with their huge flocks has had a startling impact on the northern hills where the spring-time floral displays were once glorious.

THE FORESTS OF CYPRUS

Cyprus owed some of its fame in the classical world to the dense forests which covered the land. Commercial and military ships were repaired or built here over many years, for the Persian navy and Alexander the Great through to the Venetians; timber was also exported. Even the demand for timber in mining (for pit props) and as fuel for smelting was met for centuries until, under Ottoman rule, the forests were almost exhausted by the demand for grazing land, firewood, building materials and tannin (from oak bark).

In 1974, after almost a century of restoration work by the forestry department, fire-bombing by Turkish aircraft started a conflagration which wiped out 16% of the forests. Trees are now being re-established to produce probably the best example of a sustainable forest in the Mediterranean. The Forestry College plays an important role in training students from third world countries.

Opposite: *The Cyprus crocus (*Crocus cyprius*) are the first in a succession of flowers unique to the High Troödos.*

Left: *Some of the world's oldest rocks, forced from deep inside the earth, surface in the Xeropotamos valley – a mecca for geologists.*

THE GEOMETRIC PERIOD

Pottery cups and shallow dishes decorated with bold black rings provide the inspiration for the name of a 300-year archaeological period (1050–750BC) marking the beginning of the Iron Age in Cyprus. Unusually in its history, for the first two centuries Cyprus was largely isolated because of domestic problems in neighbouring countries. It was a dark age for the island, which was plagued by major earthquakes and widespread poverty.

Below: *Petra tou Romiou, birthplace of Aphrodite, is named after the giant Romios, said to have thrown the great rocks at Arab pirates.*

HISTORY IN BRIEF

Humans have occupied Cyprus for at least 9000 years. The first settlers, thought to have voyaged from Asia Minor, lived by hunting and fishing and worshipped a 'mother goddess'. As settlement slowly spread west, locally mined **copper** was used for tools and jewellery.

The Bronze Age

Copper began to be exported from Cyprus around 2000BC. Metal weapons and other artefacts were traded with Syria, Palestine, Egypt and Minoan Crete and from 1400–1200BC Cyprus enjoyed a period of economic prosperity.

Around 1300BC Achaean Greeks from the northern Peloponnese brought their **Mycenaean** language and religious traditions. They integrated well with the locals, the cultural mix resulting in a distinctive style of pottery. They established the cities of Kition, Kourion, Pafos and Salamis and the first signs of an **Aphrodite** cult in Pafos date from this time. Severe earthquakes around 1050BC destroyed Enkomi and other late Bronze Age settlements and the island's economic fortunes foundered.

The City Kingdoms

After a long isolation the island's trade revived when **Phoenicians** from Tyre established a settlement in Kition in the 8th century BC. Other city kingdoms were established at Pafos, Amathus, Idalion, Kourion, Lapithos, Marion, Soli and Tamassos, and Cyprus prospered once again.

By 700BC the rulers of the city kingdoms had submitted to King Sargon II of **Assyria**: they paid their tribute and were largely left to rule as before. Sculpture, jewellery and pottery show an artistic flowering during the years of relative independence. On the fall of the Assyrian Empire rule passed first to the **Egyptians** in 560BC and then to the Persians in 545. **Persian** rule became increasingly harsh under Darius and all the cities except Amathus joined in the futile Ionian revolt in 499BC.

The Hellenistic Period

From 475 to 325BC the island of Cyprus remained a naval base under Persian rule. King Evagoras of Salamis, a committed Hellenophile, introduced the Greek alphabet, which gradually replaced the Cypro-Minoan script. **Alexander the Great** secured the unanimous support of the Kings of Cyprus in his campaign against the Persians and after his victory Cyprus became part of his Hellenistic empire.

Following Alexander's death in 323BC Cyprus became a pawn in the squabbles between his generals, Ptolemy and Antigonus. **Ptolemy** prevailed and Kition, Keryneia, Marion and Lapithos, the cities which had backed the wrong man, were sacked. Cyprus became thoroughly Hellenized and essentially a province of Egypt, important for its copper, timber, shipbuilding, corn and wine, with Pafos as its capital.

Above: *Sanctuary of Apollo Hylates near Lemesos.*
Below: *Early 16th-century painting of St Nestor in Agios Sozomenos, Galata.*

Pax Romana

In 58BC Cyprus was annexed by Rome, becoming a senatorial province, and a long era of peace and stability began. The apostles Paul and Barnabas arrived as missionaries in AD45 and secured an important convert in the governor, Sergius Paulus, thus making Cyprus the first country to have a **Christian** ruler. Christianity was declared the official religion in AD323, though adoption of the new faith spread slowly. Earthquakes in 332 and 365 destroyed both Pafos and Salamis, as well as most other Cypriot towns. Salamis was rebuilt as **Constantia** and became the island's capital.

Byzantium

When the Roman Empire was split in two in AD395, Cyprus came under Byzantine rule from the eastern capital, Constantinople. During the 4th and 5th centuries large basilicas were built in all the cities.

During the 7th century the coastal towns were plagued by **Arab raiders** until in 688 a treaty between Emperor Justinian II and Caliph al-Malik effectively neutralized the island, though the price of this peace was heavy taxes exacted by both the Byzantine Empire and the Caliphate.

Cyprus flourished in the Middle Byzantine period (965–1185) in spite of heavy taxation, and many towns – such as Episkopi, Famagusta, Keryneia, Lapithos and Lemesos – were either founded or enlarged. This period also saw the foundation of many prominent **churches**, including the first frescoed churches in Troödos. The **castles** of Voufavento, St Hilarion and Kantara were built as defences against future raids.

Left: *The beautiful Venetian monastery of Agia Napa is built near a spring where there had been a settlement since the Hellenistic period.*

For 10 months during 1570–71 a mixed force of 8000 Venetians and Greeks held 200,000 Ottoman troops at bay. Finally the city's resourceful Venetian commander, **Marcantonio Bragadino**, surrendered to the Ottoman Lala Mustafa Paşa. Furious at finding that he had been thwarted for so long by so few, Mustafa Paşa reneged on his solemn promises of safe passage to Crete. Bragadino was brutally tortured: his ears and nose were cut off and he was flayed alive, his skin stuffed with straw and paraded around the city.

The Lusignans and the Venetians

The despotic Isaac Comnenos declared independence from Constantinople in 1184 and began a 7-year rule characterized by greed and cruelty. In 1191 he was overthrown by **Richard the Lionheart** who was *en route* to the Third Crusade. Richard had not sought to conquer Cyprus and sold it to **Guy de Lusignan**, formerly King of Jerusalem until his ousting by Saladdin. He instituted the feudal system of his former kingdom and thus began a wonderful period for the Frankish nobility. Architecture of this period reflects their extravagant lifestyle: Byzantine castles were refurbished and cathedrals built.

Between 1374 and 1464 Famagusta was occupied by the **Genoese**, rivals of the Venetians for dominance of trade in Cyprus, whose attack on the island crippledit economically. Meanwhile, in 1426 Egyptian **Mamelukes** had sacked Larnaka and Limassol and captured King Janus. The last Lusignan monarch, James II, married the Venetian **Caterina Cornaro** in 1472. She succeeded him on his death and began a period of Venetian rule characterized by even more oppressive taxation.

Ottoman Rule

The Venetians regarded Cyprus as a frontier fortress against the threat from Ottoman forces; the decisive attack came in 1570, when Nicosia fell after a 7-week siege – with half its population slaughtered. Famagusta held out for 10 months until July 1571.

Many opulent Catholic churches were converted to mosques, but the Ottomans tolerated the **Orthodox church**, using it as an effective means of gathering taxes: those unable to pay ceded lands to the church, which retains vast holdings to this day. Over the next three centuries Muslim and Christian peasants united several times in **revolt** against punitive taxation and neglect.

The British

In the face of 19th-century Russian expansionism Britain guaranteed to protect the Ottoman Empire under the Anglo-Turkish Convention of 1878. Cyprus was leased to Britain. Turkey supported Germany in the First World War and Britain decided to annex the island, eventually declaring it a **Crown Colony** in 1925.

As the economy grew from the early 1930s so did demands for an end to British rule and for *énosis* – unity with Greece. **Makarios**, elected Bishop of Kition in 1950, became a powerful advocate of *énosis*. However, after the Suez crisis of 1954 Britain became even more determined to hang on to Cyprus, its 'unsinkable aircraft carrier'.

From 1955–59 General Grivas, a close friend and associate of Makarios, masterminded EOKA's actions in an attempt to force *énosis:* attacks on Greeks, Turks, British troops and civilians precipitated civil war in 1958. Turkey and Greece threatened to go to war, but the USA exerted pressure on both sides to find a diplomatic solution. Makarios subsequently abandoned his claim for *énosis* and Cyprus gained its **independence** but with an unsatisfactory constitution imposed upon it.

The British Legacy

Although drivers in both Greece and Turkey are encouraged to stick to the right side of the road, in Cyprus both north and south adhere to the left, part of the legacy of British colonial rule.

In the north in particular, the roads are peppered with older cars of British and continental pedigree. The climate is kind to metalwork and local mechanical ingenuity coaxes them through astonishing mileages. Village buses are all built on British lorry chassis.

English is still the second language on both sides of the divide, and the post boxes, even though they are now painted a different colour, look remarkably familiar to British visitors.

Republic of Cyprus

The constitution gave the minority Turkish population disproportionate representation in the police, army and administration. An uneasy peace existed until 1963 when Makarios proposed 13 constitutional changes. Fighting broke out in Nicosia and EOKA was revived as EOKA B: in the summer of 1964 over 500 people were killed. The Turkish Cypriots retreated into enclaves; the Greeks imposed a trade embargo, lifted in 1968.

As matters within Cyprus calmed, its relations with Athens worsened. Greek interests in America (which backed the Greek military junta) whipped up criticism of Makarios and a coalition of EOKA B and Greek military attacked the presidential palace on 15 July 1974. On 20 July the Turks bombed Nicosia and landed troops on the northern coast, and two days later the Greek Colonels fell from power in Athens. Glafkos Clerides took over as President, a position he won again in the last election.

On 14 August 1974 the Turkish army advanced: over 180,000 Greek Cypriots fled in their path. Some 37% of the island was seized in **Operation Attila** – including the main citrus growing and tourist areas – and a desperate economic crisis hit the south, which suddenly faced 40% unemployment. Bloody reprisals were inflicted on the Turks in the south, while thousands of Greek Cypriots were taken prisoner and never seen again.

After the Invasion

A near economic miracle achieved **full employment** in the south – much of it in the construction industry – by 1977. Since 1974 there have been waves of inter-communal talks and numerous United Nations resolutions deploring Turkey's occupation of the north of the island. Rauf Denktash, who has remained northern supremo since 1976, declared independence for his **Turkish Republic of Northern Cyprus** in 1983 – a state recognized by no nation other than Turkey.

Above: *The statue of Archbishop Makarios III outside the Archbishop's Palace in old Lefkosia. His name is indelibly linked with the painful birth pangs of the independent republic of Cyprus.*
Left: *The Green Line is a continuing reminder that this is, more than two decades on, still a divided island.*

GOVERNMENT AND ECONOMY

Since 1974 **Greek Cypriots**, with their innate gift for the entrepreneurial, have worked to regenerate their devastated economy. The south is now one of the wealthiest countries in the Eastern Mediterranean. Its population is highly educated (over 20 per cent have a university degree or equivalent); unemployment is under 2 per cent. The standard of health and health-care is very high: figures for life expectancy and child mortality stand favourable comparison with any western country.

The **north**, tied inextricably to Turkey's faltering economy, has not been nearly as fortunate, even though the invasion resulted in the appropriation of the main citrus growing region and the best hotels at that time. The native **Turkish Cypriots** share with their Greek counterparts the same economic aspirations, great respect for education and the living standards associated with the western world. They have little in common with the **Anatolian Turks** newly settled in Cyprus and feel, with justification, that they suffer unfavourable discrimination.

EMIGRANTS

Compared with Greek Cypriots, a high proportion of Turkish Cypriots emigrated following the invasion of 1974. About 100,000 Turkish Cypriots still live in the north, but an estimated 300,000 live in Britain, America, Australia and Turkey. A result of the invasion is that the Turks, some 18% of the population, occupy 37% of the land area.

Union with Europe

In 2004 the settlement plan put forward by UN secretary general Kofi Annan was rejected in a referendum by Greek Cypriots, while being accepted by Turkish Cypriots. The Republic of Cyprus then became a member of the European Union, leaving the Turkish-occupied North isolated. With Turkey making recent inroads in its attempts to join the European Union the political situation surrounding partition is once again coming to the fore.

Economic Renaissance

The key to the early success of the south was **tourism**; the government played the refugee card for all it was worth to attract money from outside the island, and Cyprus has become popular with many visitors from newly wealthy Eastern bloc countries. Since 1974 there has been growth in **light industry** and **manufacturing** around Lemesos. Cyprus became a base for many companies operating in the Middle East, and retains close links with the region. It is a popular base for offshore companies trading with the former Soviet republics, and a favoured holiday destination for newly wealthy Russians. Since European Union entry in 2004, the construction and property sectors have enjoyed a boom period.

The Northern Economy

In Cyprus **tourism** is inevitably a political force: the legal government has been highly vocal in pointing out that, under international law, many northern hotels were illegally appropriated and that tourists are therefore colluding in the illegal occupation. However, a Cyprus which has remained largely unchanged since 1974 and in which tourism is in its infancy is appealing, and the beauty of the north combined with the friendly welcome of the Turkish Cypriots attracts a small but enthusiastic market.

Growth in **agriculture**, has been severely hampered because fruit exports and juice production were tied to the misfortunes of Mr Asil Nadir: the collapse of his Polly Peck empire after its meteoric rise proved temporarily devastating to the northern economy.

GETTING AROUND

A limited motorway network connects Lemesos with Lefkosia and Larnaka, and on to Pafos. It is currently being upgraded with financial assistance from the European Union. The volume of heavily laden lorries using the coast road to Pafos can make the going rather slow during the working day. Driving in Cyprus is further spiced by taxi drivers executing hair-raising moves in order to ply their trade.

Good fast roads connect the Troödos region with Lefkosia and with Lemesos in the south: but these roads are also often congested by heavy lorries.

For the visitor with a hire car a special attraction is the network of narrow cobbled roads weaving their way across the landscape, plus an even more extensive system of forestry roads leading well into the back of beyond.

After winter rains, roads can become quite heavily rutted and hard going even for four-wheel drive; by summer many of them have been smoothed by the bulldozers of the forestry department skimming off the surface irregularities.

Opposite: *Hotels large and small and tourism in general have greatly contributed to the meteoric recovery in the Cypriot economy.*
Left: *A roadside orange-seller in Pafos.*

THE PEOPLE

Thanks to a long and chequered history, Cypriots do not fall into definite racial categories so much as groups distinguished by their linguistic and religious allegiances. The different elements within the population – Greeks, Latins and Turks – have always mixed and matched.

Although there was a faint hope that Glafkos Clerides and Rauf Denktash might achieve agreement between the largest of the groups, the Greek speakers of the south and the Turkish speakers of the north, many resignedly accept the *status quo* and turn to national pride for comfort.

Both **Turkish** and **Greek Cypriots** are quite different from their respective mainland counterparts, but are very much like each other in terms of human warmth and **hospitality**. A genuine friendliness is something on which everyone who visits Cyprus is likely to comment, even if at the height of summer it is not so obvious when the south is overrun by tourists. Turkish Cypriots are, on the whole, more reticent than extrovert Greek Cypriots, but they possess great charm and warmth. What keeps these communities apart is politics.

> **AN AGRICULTURAL NICHE**
>
> Despite being outside the EU until recently, the Cypriot climate and growing skills have allowed the republic to exploit several market niches. The production of early vegetables avoided conflict with EU quotas, and 'exotica' such as avocados have flourished for some time. Guavas and mangoes are now being grown too. One relative newcomer to the list of crops is fenugreek, exported to satisfy the discerning taste of affluent Asian communities in Europe.

Education

Compulsory school begins at 5½ often followed almost immediately by private lessons in English and, to a lesser extent, other languages. The work ethic is strong in Cypriot children. Entry to the **Gymnasium** is at 11, followed by a division after three years into academic and technical streams. In all the main towns there are private international schools (such as the English School and the Falcon School in Lefkosia). These cater for children of all nationalities and prepare them for entry to both British and American universities. The insatiable thirst for qualifications has spawned an industry in 'crammers' (*frontisteria*). The **University**

of Cyprus, long awaited, opened in 1992 with a limited range of courses and plans for many more. It has an excellent reputation though many students go abroad to study – to Britain, the USA, Canada, France or Germany – since Cyprus is too small an island to provide enough employment for qualified professionals.

Family Life

The importance of the **family** overrides everything else to a Cypriot: ties are strong and consequently people feel they matter to one another and crime levels are very low. Cypriots genuinely love **children** and cannot understand the reports they read of child abuse elsewhere. The extended family is instrumental in enabling many professional women in Cyprus to continue their careers, leaving their children under the wing of 'Yia-ya' (grandmother) and their aunts.

Wherever a Cypriot ends up, great **loyalty** is always felt to 'my village'. Many professionals return to second homes at weekends where they grow fruit and vegetables, a way of retaining something of the old life. They are not the only part-time growers: it has long been difficult to attract highly educated young Cypriots back to the **land** full time, and many 'farmers' tend their produce in addition to their main jobs in the cities. In recent years, acute labour shortages have resulted in the recruitment of agricultural and hotel labour from former communist bloc countries, as well as recently from Felcon New EU States.

It is dangerous to categorize people by appearance, either in the south or the north: an old gentleman in his traditional baggy trousers, tanned and wrinkled like an

Above: *Women literally form the backbone of the traditional rural workforce.*
Opposite: *The village café remains a male preserve where politics are mulled over and deals clinched on a handshake.*

THE PACKAGE TRADE

A very large proportion of visitors to Cyprus book all-inclusive holidays, making it difficult for the independent traveller to arrive in summer and find accommodation 'on spec'. In the five winter months (November–March) the situation is different, although the proportion of visitors arriving at this time of year (around 20%) is gradually getting higher. Just over 25% of all visitors arrive during the two 'peak' months of July and August.

DIFFERENT FAITHS

Among the resident population of about 650,000 religious adherence is divided: 84% of the people are members of the Greek Orthodox church, 14% are Muslims, and the remaining 2% are Maronite, Armenian or Catholic. Settlers in the north are not included these statistics since no official figures are quoted.

olive, may well have one son who is a professor in Boston, another a surgeon in London and an economist daughter. Both Greek and Turkish Cypriots are much more **cosmopolitan** than they may appear at first sight: most will have travelled abroad and nearly everyone seems to have relatives in London.

Every summer village populations are swollen by '**returnees**': Cypriots who have made good in London, Sydney or New York. In Drousia the annual influx was so great that they built a hotel to cope – the Drousia Heights (*see p. 49*). Here and elsewhere the young people speaking in broad London or Sydney accents one minute will then turn effortlessly to the village Greek they have always used at home.

Both communities appear to be **male-dominated**: in the north the coffee shops are an indisputable male preserve; in the south, foreign females entering to buy coffee or a drink may be greeted with a slightly bemused look, but never with antipathy. Beneath the surface, however, male domination is far from the case in Greek Cypriot families: mothers have fought to make sure that daughters get the same educational advantages as sons.

The **dowry system** prevails, usually involving the provision of a home for the young couple. It gives the children a marvellous start and is largely built into the expectations of everyone's lives. Many families will build above their own homes (hence the plethora of unfinished houses, with reinforcement rods standing proud awaiting the extra storey) and take on extra jobs to fulfil this obligation.

Religion

Religion is important in Cyprus but is not usually a contentious issue. The south is Greek Orthodox and the north Sunni Muslim, but within both areas are other religious adherences as well as secular groups.

Cyprus has long had an Armenian community, largely involved in business. They live in

Left: *Restored frescoes glow in the cathedral of Agios Ioannis in Lefkosia.*
Opposite: *A game of* tavli, *or backgammon is being enjoyed at a Cypriot café.*

the main towns of the south, having been expelled from the north. There are also Latins, descendants of Lusignan and Venetian families, and Maronites who have very limited access to their former villages in the north. Lebanese and other immigrants into the south adhere to their Islamic faith and there are mosques in all the large towns. In southern villages the priest is a familiar sight sitting in the local café, pivotal in the community and aware of everything, good and bad, going on amongst his flock.

Art and Culture

The architectural legacy of past times is evident in all the major towns: **Byzantine** churches and fortifications were expanded by **Lusignan** rulers, fortified by the **Venetians** and then rebuilt by Ottoman **Turks**. The main towns and cities have all suffered from the use and abuse of the 'great god concrete', particularly following the invasion, when planning controls may have existed but were not implemented. Sadly, many fine old houses have disappeared, though some **Ottoman** and early **colonial** buildings have survived: fortunately protection of architectural treasures is now much stronger.

The island's museums hold ample evidence, in the

Above: *A bouzouki player: groups performing in large hotels and restaurants include traditional Cypriot tunes in their repertoire as well as the inevitable 'Zorba's Dance'.*
Opposite: *Skiing in Cyprus is for fun rather than for serious enthusiasts.*

TRADITIONAL MUSIC

Traditional folk songs are often played in 7/8 time, and Cypriot musicians cope easily with changes between 2/4, 9/8, 5/8 and 6/8. Scales correspond to the Aeolian and Doric modes used in the music of the early church. In the Orthodox church only chants are allowed: the Armenian church, on the other hand, has a rich tradition of music dating back to the 6th century, much of it hauntingly beautiful.

---

form of **ceramics**, **statuary** and **jewellery**, of the importance of art in successive cultural epochs. **Mosaics** show changes from pagan to Christian influences, as geometric patterns supplant floral and animal motifs. One of the most remarkable aspects of the artistic heritage of Cyprus is the abundance of **painted churches**, where wall paintings and icons span the styles of the 10th to 17th centuries.

Music and Dance

Young people in Cyprus, both north and south, are as well-informed as any in the western world about the various categories of rock and pop music. The national radio stations play Greek (and Turkish) music. In the south, **traditional music** – usually the light, rhythmical tunes of *tsiftetelis* and *rembetiko* – is kept alive by determined groups of musicians who perform at weddings and various festivals, or for dances.

Traditional **dances** are elegant, with an emphasis on economy of movement, the outstretched arms lending balance. Even 'gravitationally challenged' Cypriot men can muster an instinctive grace which visitors roped in to dance find difficult to match.

Turkish Cypriot music is indistinguishable from mainland Turkish music: the *sas*, a lute-like instrument with several drone strings, is particularly popular.

Sport and Recreation

Local sporting passions are directed largely towards **football** and **tennis**. Resorts in the south cater for a variety of **watersports**, from swimming and scuba diving to windsurfing and parascending. In the north, windsurfing and other facilities are concentrated near Keryneia and Salamis.

There are plenty of opportunities to watch or participate in **tennis**, with numerous private clubs and hotel courts. **Hiking** is being promoted by the CTO: given the vast network of mountain trails and reasonably predictable weather in spring and autumn. The northern hills are ideal for hikers, but involve dodging the rather ubiquitous military camps. **Mountain biking** is taking off in Cyprus and could become very popular indeed. In September, the **Cyprus Motor Rally** attracts a lot of interest, both local and international – especially since points are gained for the European Championship.

In winter the Troödos offers **skiing**: three lifts on the northeast face of Mount Olympus open from late December to March or early April. **Golfers** will find an 18-hole, par 72 golf course near Pafos and Lemesos.

Horse riding centres are scattered throughout the island and an annual **kite flying** festival is organised in the first week of March by the Pafos municipality.

THE CYPRUS RALLY

Held each year in September, the Cyprus Rally attracts both locally based and well-known international competitors to an event with increasing prestige and great national support. The race begins in Lefkosia and moves quickly onto the winding roads and tracks of the Troödos mountains. Every stage is very well planned and marked so that the non-racing driver has no risk of getting caught up in a nightmare.

VEGETARIAN FOOD

The Greek word for vegetarian is *hortophagos* – 'grass eater' – which, of course, speaks volumes. Apparently vegetarian fare, such as pilaffs of bulgur wheat, may have been cooked in chicken stock (not really meat...). And even *koupepia/dolmas* (vine leaves stuffed with rice and pine nuts) sometimes include some minced meat in the Cypriot version – ask before ordering.

Food and Drink

Most people experience Cypriot food through endless alfresco meals: meat (*kebap* or *kleftiko*) or fish (grilled or fried), a large portion of *patates* (chips, with lemon juice rather than vinegar) and the ubiquitous *khoriatiki salata*, peasant salad like the Greek version but with the addition of pickled capers (*kapari/gebre*) complete with stems and leaves. Cypriot cuisine, sometimes hard to find outside a Cypriot home, has a heritage of interesting dishes, many of them vegetarian.

The **meze**, literally 'mixture', is an experience to be taken with a loose-fitting waistband: dishes (twenty or so) keep coming to the table, starting with dips and followed by a variety of dishes according to what is available. Better restaurants have realised that discerning visitors enjoy traditional Cypriot dishes so more of these are beginning to appear in *mezedes*.

Traditional Greek and Turkish fare is identical in nature and often close in name. **Starters** include *hummus/humus* (chick pea dip), *taramas/tarama* made with smoked cod's roe, *talatouri/cacik* (yoghurt with mint and cucumber), *tahine/tahin* (creamy sesame paste with lemon) and *elies/zeytin*, green olives with crushed garlic and cracked coriander seeds.

'Peasant' **vegetable dishes** are often delicious stews, such as *louvia me kolokithakia/burulce* (black-eyed beans with courgettes in lemon juice and olive oil) and *bamies/bamya* (okra in tomato sauce). *Trahanas/tarhana* is a dried 'biscuit' of bulgur

wheat and yoghurt, added to soup with the local **cheese**, *halloumi*. For self-caterers the quality of local vegetables in the south is superb. Wonderfully flavoured tomatoes, peppers, aubergines, artichokes and avocados abound.

Eggs (*avga/yumurta*) are often cooked in a sort of loose omelette using whatever happens to be in season. In autumn this may be wild mushrooms, in spring, thin wild asparagus or *strouthia* ('little sparrows'), the leaves and shoots of bladder campion.

Fish tends to be quite expensive because catches around the island are rather small. Certainly worth trying are:

barbouuni/barbun (grilled red mullet), *maridhes/gopes* (fried whitebait) and *xifia* (sword-fish marinated in oil and lemon and grilled). Deep-fried squid (*kala marakia/kalamar*) are excellent when fresh caught, but most restaurant fare comes frozen from the Far East.

The expectation of **meat** at every meal has grown with prosperity and now meat is usually what hosts feel guests should be served. Meat dishes include *hiromeri* (cured ham), *keftedes/kofte* (meatballs), *loundza* (smoked pork), *souvlakia/şiş kebap* (grilled kebabs) and *sheftalia/şeftalia* (grilled sausages). *Kleftiko/küp kebap* is ostensibly lamb cooked for hours in its own juice in a sealed clay oven: this technique tenderizes even the most ancient sheep or goat meat. *Tavas/tava* is a stew made with beef or rabbit and lots of onions.

Cyprus has long been famous for its citrus **fruit**, but in season there are also apples, pears, apricots, peaches, nectarines, tiny bananas from the west, strawberries, grapes, figs, melons and pomegranates. The cherry season is short but well worth travelling to Cyprus for: try the traditional *glyka* – fruits in syrup (*see p. 61*).

Many **cakes and pastries** are seasonal, baked to accompany a religious festival, such as *flaounes* (a yeast turnover filled with raisins, eggs and cheese) for Easter and *vassilopitta* (yeast dough spread with egg, almonds and sesame seeds) for Christmas. Useful lunchtime or picnic standbys are pasties made with filo pastry: *tiropitta*, filled with minted cheese (either *feta* or *halloumi*), *spanachopitta* with spinach and cheese or *eliopitta* with black olives. Cypriots have a sweet tooth and love pastries soaked in sugar syrup: *baklava* is nut-filled puff pastry, *daktila* arefilo fingers with a nut and cinnamon filling, and *loukoumades* are deep-fried balls of choux pastry.

Above: *Town markets offer an unbeatable source of fruit, vegetables and general provisions for self-caterers and often sell good locally made crafts rather than tourist 'tat'.*

Opposite: *Souvlakia (kebabs) are as much part of the holiday experience in Cyprus as the sunshine.*

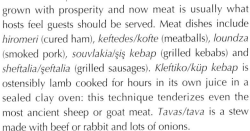

For many visitors, *halloumi* (*hellim*) is their food discovery in Cyprus. This rather rubbery cheese is, like *feta* (*beyaz panir*), made from goat's or sheep's milk; mint is pressed into it and it is stored in its own whey. Cut in thin slices it can be eaten as it is, grilled or even fried for those with a contempt for calories. The supermarket product is good but village *halloumi* is an experience not to be missed.

Right: *Home-made retsina is served at the Svarna Tavern near Protaras.*

Honey, usually of the very runny kind, is a great favourite and is often served poured over creamy fresh yoghurt or with *anari*, a soft white cheese which is a by-product of *halloumi*-making. *Soutsoukou* is a long string of almonds coated by soaking in a concoction of grape juice, flour and rosewater and then dried. *Loukoumia* (Turkish delight, diplomatically called Cyprus delight in the south) has long been a local speciality.

Drinks

Freshly prepared fruit juices are readily available in the island. Water is also a great favourite: Cypriots take a connoisseur's attitude towards water from the mountains.

Several good (and cheap) **brandies** are produced, including a VSOP – a favourite tipple with locals in cafés. Visitors encounter it as a 'brandy sour', virtually the national drink, mixed with ice, lemon juice, angostura bitters and soda water: beware – in the heat, these slip down easily and rising from the table suddenly becomes a problem.

Ouzo (aniseed-flavoured spirit) is served locally with iced water and slices of cucumber. *Filfar* is an orange liqueur, marvellous as a nightcap. Visitors might be offered 'Cyprus whiskey' in an assortment of 'pre-owned' bottles: this is *zivania*, a fire-water. Treated with care it can restore life to frozen extremities after winter walking or skiing, either by being imbibed or as a rub... One northern distillery produces *raki*.

Beers of lager type are brewed on the island: Carlsberg (under franchise) and Keo.

Mosaics in Pafos show that **wine** growing and drinking have long been associated with Aphrodite's isle, although you will never see Cypriots the worse for wear in public. The climate and soils are ideal for viticulture: village wines, still obtainable direct from huge terracotta vessels (*pithari*), are of variable quality, the best being highly quaffable. In recent years, young Australians (often from *émigré* Cypriot families) have imported the fastidiousness that Antipodean wine-makers use in their own production and Cyprus wine is rapidly changing for the better. The dessert wine, Commandaria, has long been famed (*see p. 73*).

Traditionally, the main Cyprus grapes are Xynisteri (the native white grape) and Mavron (the black grape of Greece) but experiments are being carried out with others. North Cyprus has so far failed to produce any wines of quality, and most restaurant wine is imported from Turkey.

Cheap Cyprus **sherry** has an unfortunate image as the mainstay of the tippler. However, Cyprus dry sherries, served very cold, can take their place with the best.

HOW DO YOU LIKE YOUR COFFEE

In Cyprus you have two alternatives. **Nescafé** is a generic term for any instant coffee, usually served in a sachet with a pot of tepid water for do-it-yourselfers. Traditional coffee, a finely ground mocha boiled in a small pot and served unfiltered in small cups, is called **Cyprus coffee** in the south and **Turkish coffee** north of the Attila line.

Those with a sweet tooth should ask for *kafés glykos*; medium is *metrios* and unsweetened *sketos* or *pikros* (the Turkish equivalents are *sekerli*, *orta* and *sade*, respectively). Local connoisseurs recognize intermediate stages. Both north and south, coffee is served with a glass of cold water.

Below: *The old buildings of Lefkosia's Laïki Geitonia have been restored and now house shops and restaurants.*

2
Pafos and the West

For decades, **Pafos** remained a backwater, escaping the urban development of Nicosia and Lemesos. But in 1984 an airport was built to the east of Pafos and hotels rapidly spread out from the town to greet it. These days Pafos, with its year-round sunshine, is most renowned as a tourist resort. This does it something of a disservice as it also enjoys a place on UNESCO's World Heritage list with some of the finest Roman mosaics and Greek ruins that you will ever see. It is still easy to leave the bustling town behind and find a very different Cyprus.

The first settlement, **Palea Pafos**, was established around 1500BC, and the present town, **Nea Pafos**, was founded in the 4th century BC by King Nikokles as a port for the older city. Conquered by the Ptolemies in 312BC, it flourished under their rule, becoming the island's capital in the 2nd century BC. Further prosperity followed during the Pax Romana after 58BC, when it became the seat of the Roman Proconsul. In the 4th century AD the city was destroyed by an earthquake and power transferred to the city kingdom of Salamis, under its new name **Constantia**.

Pafos retained its reputation for shipbuilding, however, and ships put in for supplies and refitting during the Crusades. **Ktima**, the upper town, was built following attacks from Arab invaders, but Nea Pafos was not entirely deserted and it briefly flourished again as a port under Lusignan and Venetian rule. In Ottoman times it was gradually deserted. Nowadays the coastal strip to the east is awash with hotels, banks and restaurants.

DON'T MISS

*** Akamas Peninsula: walk in the island's first national park.
** Mosaics: the ancient Roman **mosaics** of Pafos.
** Tombs of the Kings.
* Arodes, Drouseia and **Kritou:** picturesque mountain villages.
* Chrysorrogiatissa: visit the ancient monastery.

Opposite: *The dramatic north coast of Cyprus is still off the main tourist track and is wild and surprisingly unspoiled.*

Below: *The fort guarding Pafos harbour.*

NEA PAFOS ★★★

Pafos' bustling **harbour** has retained its appeal, with many fish restaurants and a tame pelican strutting along the waterfront. The small **castle** (open Monday to Friday 07:30–19:30, until sunset October–May) guarding the harbour entrance is all that remains of a larger Lusignan building dating from 1391. Demolished by the Venetians to prevent its use by invading Turks, it was rebuilt under Ottoman rule. Boat trips (excursions in a glass-bottomed boat) go from the harbour to Lara and around Akamas.

The ruins of **Nea Pafos** are bounded by the remains of the city wall and cover an area of 95ha (235 acres) north of the harbour. The site is on the UNESCO list of world monuments, and even garden walls in the back streets here include 'recycled' chunks of stone columns.

Saranda Colones ★★

Just to the west of the road leading from the harbour (Apostolou Pavlou) are the remains of a Lusignan castle built over a 7th-century Byzantine fortification. Destroyed in the 13th century by an earthquake, it is named after the 40 ('*saranda*') broken granite columns found on the site.

The Mosaics ★★★

Pafos is famed for its floor mosaics dating from the 2nd and 3rd centuries AD, which lie in houses named after the principal characters depicted (open daily, 07:30–19:30, until sunset October–May). The **House of Dionysos** mosaics celebrate wine-drinking, the most famous being the Triumph of Dionysos, in which the god is riding in a chariot drawn by

leopards accompanied by his inebriated followers. In the **House of Orpheus** one mosaic depicts Orpheus with his lyre surrounded by admirers. Discovered only in 1992, the **House of the Four Seasons**, with its hunting scenes, is still under excavation. The **House of Aion** has a panel showing Aion, judge of all mankind, ruling on a beauty contest between sea nymphs. The **House of Theseus**, perhaps the Roman governor's house, contains a mosaic displaying the fight between Theseus and the Cretan Minotaur, the legendary half-man, half-bull.

The Odeion ★

North of the mosaics, near the **lighthouse**, this small, 2nd-century Roman theatre was damaged by an earthquake and finally abandoned in the 7th century. It has been partly restored. It is connected by corridor to the **Asklepeion** (centre of healing), and nearby lie the bases of Corinthian columns which show the position of the **Agora** (marketplace). All that remains of

Above: The Pafos Odeion and lighthouse.

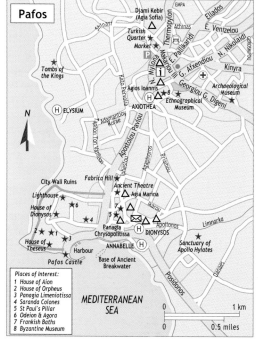

Pafos

Places of Interest:
1 House of Aion
2 House of Orpheus
3 Panagia Limeniotissa
4 Saranda Colones
5 St Paul's Pillar
6 Odeion & Agora
7 Frankish Baths
8 Byzantine Museum

MOSAIC DESIGN

Mosaic floors graced the houses of wealthy Romans and public buildings such as communal baths. The best mosaics were formed from cubes of coloured glass (*tesserae*), sometimes with gold leaf applied; others employed cubes of coloured stone. Pre-Christian mosaics depict scenes taken from tales of the Greek gods and heroes. Later compositions were laid over the earlier versions, with the influence of Christianity showing up in geometric designs and floral motifs. In general, human subjects are shown full-face, but animals, pagans and the wicked appear in profile. Originally mosaics were kept highly polished, appearing much brighter than they do now.

Below: *The Phoenician tombs in Pafos were never the last resting-place of royalty but their sheer scale has led to their being called the Tombs of the Kings.*

a **Hellenistic altar** are foundations plus a set of steps: evidence has been found in Pafos that in addition to Aphrodite, Apollo, Artemis and Zeus were worshipped.

The Catacombs ★

Other parts of Nea Pafos lie to the east of the main road where it merges with Kato Pafos. Numerous chambers have been cut into the soft rocks below Ktima: two underground rooms, probably cut in the 4th century BC, form the **Guards' Camp** just inside the city wall. **Fabrica Hill**, near the large as yet unexcavated **Theatre**, houses a complex of underground rooms. Two catacombs are visible: **Agia Solomoni** is marked by a tree with numerous offerings tied to it; **Agia Lambrianos** now has a garden in front of it. Many locals still believe in the restorative powers of the catacombs but in Pafos it is never clear which lady – the Panagia (the Virgin Mary) or the much older Aphrodite – is expected to answer the prayers.

The Tombs of the Kings ★★

The tombs date from the Ptolemaic period, and lie just off the road heading north out of Pafos towards Coral Bay. No royalty was actually buried here, but with about 100 tombs found on the headland the site's scale is impressive.

Behind a façade of Doric columns, the tombs are cut out of rock, and those arranged around a subterranean 'courtyard' are particularly grand. Open daily, 08:30–19:30 in summer, until sunset in winter.

Agia Kiriaki ★

The area just to the east of Apostolou Pavlou is the place to search for **Byzantine** and earlier churches.

Above: *Chrysopolitissa basilica with its mosaic floors is also the site of the pillar at which St Paul is said to have been flogged.*

Chrysopolitissa was one of the earliest Christian basilicas to be built in the island, dating from the 4th century. The original building had seven aisles and many columns remain. Three of the early floor mosaics show scenes from the Old Testament but later floors used plant and geometrical designs. The basilica was destroyed in the 7th century by Arab invaders. A small church built on the site was demolished and the church of **Agia Kyriaki**, currently used by both Catholic and Anglican expatriates, was built in 1500. **St Paul's Pillar** stands at the far end of the site. Nea Pafos became the seat of the Bishops of Pafos during the Lusignan and Venetian periods. The remains of the **Franciscan church** with its twin arches above a double column lie to the northeast of Agia Kyriaki, with a series of Frankish (Lusignan) tombs nearby.

The Market and the Turkish Quarter ★

Pafos has all the shops, banks and facilities you would expect from a popular tourist resort. Many gift shops sell 'tat' but, for the more discerning, there are several outlets for local craftspeople. The **covered market** in Ktima sells locally produced wares as well as fresh produce. Much of Ktíma is dedicated to the tourist, but worth exploring is the former **Turkish quarter** (a protected enclave until 1974) with its narrow streets and the **Djami Kebir mosque**, once the Byzantine church of Agia Sofia.

> ### EARLY CONVERT
>
> The Apostles Paul and Barnabas visited Pafos in AD47 and succeeded in converting Sergius Paulus, the Proconsul of the time, to the new faith of Christianity. However, they achieved this success only after the locals had made sure Paul suffered for his beliefs: the church of **Agia Kyriaki** contains the pillar against which he is said to have received 39 lashes.

APHRODITE AND CYPRUS

According to the poet **Homer**, Aphrodite was the 'Cyprian': the goddess who emerged fully grown from the foaming sea at **Petra tou Romiou** (Aphrodite's Rocks) near Palea Pafos. She is also associated with a much earlier eastern deity, **Astarte**, who demanded human sacrifice and evolved into **Venus**, the Roman goddess of love. Aphrodite was also linked with battle through her support of the Trojans. However, when wounded by Diomedes the *Iliad* records that she was reminded by a politically incorrect Zeus to 'make love, not war'. At Amathus and in other towns Aphrodite was worshipped as a bearded man, **Aphroditus**.

Pafos Museums ★★

Two of the town's museums are sited close to the Central Park. The small **Byzantine Museum** (open Monday–Friday 09:00–12:30 and 14:00–17:00; 16:00–19:00 June–September; Saturday mornings only) is a must for those interested in icons and other religious works of art. The privately run **Ethnographical Museum** (open Monday–Saturday 09:00–18:00 and Sunday 09:00–13:00; September, Saturday mornings only) houses the idiosyncratic but fascinating collection of George Eliades. It has a strong archaeological content in addition to collections of dress and domestic implements.

A wealth of local finds is displayed in the **Pafos Archaeological Museum** (open Monday–Friday 09:00–14:30, Thursday 15:00–18:00, weekends 10:00–13:00), some distance to the east of town on the main road to the airport (Grivas Digenis). All the periods of Cypriot history, from Neolithic and Chalcolithic onwards, are represented. Of particular note are the statues of **Asklepios** and Egyptian **Isis**, extensive collections of **coinage** and **pottery** and a gruesome collection of Roman **surgical tools**.

Geroskipou ★★

Travelling southeast from Pafos, Geroskipou lies on the route once taken by festive processions of young men and women from Nea Pafos to Palea Pafos (*hieros kipos* means 'sacred grove'). The church of **Agia Paraskevi** is unique in having five tiled domes. Decorations over its altar date from the 9th century, while the earliest fresco dates from the 10th century. There is a **Folk Art Museum** in the house of Hadji Smith, open Monday–Friday, 7:30–14:30, also Thursday 15:00–18:00 except July and August.

The village is well known for its crafts, with stalls and shops along the main street selling pottery, basketware and **loukoumia** (Turkish delight, though it is prudent to ask for Cyprus delight).

Palea Pafos ★★

The village of **Kouklia**, 11km (7 miles) east of Geroskipou, stands on the site of Palea Pafos. Its Lusignan manor, **La Cavocle**, is visible from the main road. Much of the building dates from the Ottoman period but in Crusader days it was surrounded by sugar-cane plantations. The manor is now a museum and houses finds from the adjacent site.

Little remains of ancient Pafos: the **Sanctuary of Aphrodite** (open Monday–Friday 07:30–17:00, weekends 09:00–16:00) comprises a hotchpotch of ruins spanning late Bronze Age to Roman times, but successive sets of local inhabitants have seen it as a convenient source of cut stone, from builders of a Roman villa to the foundations for medieval sugar-milling machinery. A walk around the village reveals carved stones incorporated in the walls of the older houses. A **necropolis** is under excavation to the southeast of the hill, while on the road to **Pano Archimandrita** are the remains of a siege ramp and city gate built by the Persians during the Ionian revolt of 498BC. The church of **Panagia Katholiki** dates from the 12th century.

The road to Pano Archimandrita and beyond offers spectacular panoramas and a route into the chalky hills of **vine-growing** southern Troödos. Signposted to the south of the village is the hermitage of **Agia Pateres**: preserved in a rock shrine are bones, said to be those of 318 saints who were killed at Pissouri after fleeing Syria.

Above: *La Cavocle, a Lusignan manor, dominates the much earlier site of Palea Pafos at Kouklia.* **Opposite:** *The church of Agia Paraskevi is in the centre of Geroskipou.*

THE OLDEST PROFESSION

The first temple dedicated to Aphrodite was built by the priest-king Kinyras at Palea Pafos in the 12th century BC. The cult of Aphrodite flourished in old Pafos and Herodotus mentions that **temple prostitution** was an established practice. It was the custom for young women to surrender their 'virginity' within the temple precincts to whomsoever happened to be passing at the time. Any proceeds from these 'sacrificial' encounters were dedicated to the goddess. Spring celebrations dedicated to Aphrodite attracted pilgrims from afar.

GRIVAS MUSEUM

It is now hard to believe
that it was the isolation
of the west coast of Cyprus
that led it to be used as a
landing-place by EOKA
forces. Near **Chlorakas**,
just north of Pafos, the
Grivas Museum houses the
boat in which the general
landed nearby in 1954.

THE WEST COAST
The Avagas Gorge ★★

From the coastal road beyond **Agios Georgios**, north of
Pafos, tracks climb through a landscape of spectacular valleys cut by rivers flowing to
the sea. Although parts of
the route may be nego-
tiable by four-wheel drive
vehicles the only way to
appreciate this unspoiled
part of the island is on foot.
In summer, a sun hat and a
supply of water is essential;
in spring and autumn walking is comfortable and the
chance of meeting anyone
else is very remote. The
Avagas Gorge (from *avga*,
meaning eggs, supposedly
collected from the cliffs for
food) has a special allure –
the sculpted rock walls
close in on a valley seldom
penetrated by the sun's
rays. It is a scramble (two
hours plus) up through the
gorge to **Kato Arodes**; alternatively, a downhill trek
can be started here.

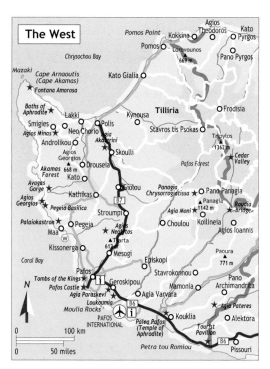

The West

The West Coast Road ★

The road from Pafos along the west coast offers an interesting alternative route to **Polis**, worth incorporating as part of a round trip. Near the coast the road skirts banana plantations with blue plastic sacks covering the ripening fruit. **Coral Bay**, with its expanse of sandy beach, has become a popular resort with a large complex of hotels, apartments, shops and restaurants. Northwest of the beach lies a fascinating coast with bizarre white 'moonscapes' formed from wave-sculpted chalk rocks, sea caves and, below **Agios Georgios**, tombs cut in the cliffs.

Geronisos Island, with a Neolithic settlement and Roman ruins, lies off Agios Georgios but the latter, 20km (12 miles) from Pafos, is best known for its domed church – a landmark on the headland. On the clifftop (**Cape Drepano**) there are ruins dating from the 11th to 14th centuries as well as the outline of a 6th-century basilica with mosaic floors and a Bronze Age site (**Maa**).

Beyond Agios Georgios the road to Lara (see p. 46) is rutted, but a good road cuts inland through banana plantations to **Pegeia**, a hillside village with good tavernas in its square. The road climbs through woods of Aleppo pine (**Pegeia Forest**) where in spring the ground is a carpet of anemones and orchids, though by June it is brown and dry. **Kathikas** sits on top of the Akamas Peninsula (see p. 46), and from here the road to Polis winds through unspoiled villages. Accommodation in village houses is available as part of the Laona Project (see p. 48).

(see p. 46), (see p. 46), (see p. 48)

NEOPHYTOS THE PEOPLE'S SAINT

Neophytos came from his native Lefkara at the age of 25 and settled as a hermit in a wooded valley 9km (6 miles) to the north of Pafos in 1159. Tradition holds that with his bare hands he cut the three caves in the hillside rock which comprise his hermitage. Some of the paintings on the interior rock were done under his supervision and are important for their two distinct styles: the neo-classical style of artists from Constantinople, working in 1183, and the typical contemporary style of the frescoes dating from 1196.

Neophytos was regarded as a folk hero for the tracts he wrote openly condemning Byzantine tax collectors and exposing oppressive conditions on the island. Caves higher on the cliff face are where the hermit is said to have retreated when his popularity became too much for him to bear.

The monastery of **Agios Neofytos**, near the caves, was founded in 1220.

Left and opposite:
Along the lonely coast north of Coral Bay the sea has sculpted the soft white chalk into a bizarre landscape of arches and columns.

POLIS

The town's full name, **Polis Chrysochou**, means 'city of the golden land', but golden is not quite the impression gained on arrival here. This small town with its slightly shabby façade has a distinct neglected charm and a drowsy air of its own which was, until recently, sampled mainly by backpackers and other independent travellers. Increased wealth from tourism has brought benefits, such as a lick of paint on the houses, the establishment of a pedestrian area with cafés, pensions and rooms to rent, and a puzzling one-way system. Some locals fear that the current level of hotel and holiday home construction is threatening to destroy Polis' charm.

The **Turkish** influence evident in the old stone buildings gives them architectural appeal: many of the town houses have ornate doorways through which you may catch a glimpse of the interior arches beyond. A sense of peace in present-day Polis belies a turbulent past: in the early days of the British administration its reputation was for lawlessness, with pirates and slave-traders plying their trade along the coast, while highwaymen imperilled travellers on land. Until 1974 there was a UN post in Polis because of bitter strife between the Turkish Cypriots of the surrounding villages and the strongly pro-*énosis* Greek community in the town.

The Byzantine church of **Agios Andronikos**, in common with many other churches, was taken over by the Ottoman Turks and used as a mosque until the evacuation of the Turkish Cypriot population. Since then, the 16th-century frescoes have been painstakingly cleaned by archaeologists from the Department of Antiquities.

Right: *A solitary church stands in a wild area of small vineyards and scrub-covered hills south of Polis.*

Left: *One of the last wild places in the island, the potential of Akamas is realized by conservationists and developers alike – only time will tell who will win.*

Beaches near Polis ★

Polis is within easy reach of pleasant, if not wonderful, beaches – the sand is dark, not white or golden – often backed by citrus groves which have been extended dramatically as Polis has grown in importance as a citrus-producing centre following the loss of Morfou to the east. The large **campsite** is set amidst eucalyptus trees about 1.5km (1 mile) north of the town. The coves along the north coast, with their dark sand and even darker rocks, are reasonably secluded, except in the months of July and August when they become a place of escape for Cypriots.

Stroumpi ★

This prosperous village famous for its wine and sultanas lies astride the mountain ridge separating Polis and Pafos; in 1953 it was badly hit by an earthquake. The easiest route to **Chrysorrogiatissa** (and **Panagia**) begins here, just south of the village. In early April the distant scarlet haze below the fruit trees is in reality a sea of **wild tulips**. Enterprising youngsters try to sell bunches to tourists – in spite of, or perhaps because of this trade, they survive. Without the small income the locals might be tempted to plough the land and destroy the bulbs.

MARION AND ARSINOË

Copper provided the economic basis for an export trade on which the ancient kingdom of Marion grew rich. Founded in the 7th century BC by Ionian Greeks, Marion was destroyed by Ptolemy I in 312BC. What little remains of the settlement of Marion lies just outside Polis (roughly to the northeast) and is hard to find. There are thousands of tombs in the area where, at the end of the 19th century, enterprising robbers found rich pickings, supplying collectors and museums abroad. The town of Arsinoë, named after the wife of one of the Ptolemies, replaced Marion but was sited slightly towards the west, where present-day Polis lies. Arsinoë became one of the ten city kingdoms of Cyprus and excavations are still continuing.

Panagia Chrysorrogiatissa ★★

This monastery owes its Christian foundation in 1192 to the hermit **Ignatius.** One legend says he was told in a dream to build a church on the site, while another relates to the discovery of a miraculous icon (painted by St Luke). The name literally means 'Our Lady of the Golden Pomegranates': the fruits being symbolic of, and a slang term for, breasts, it is hard to ignore a possible link with the goddess Aphrodite who is often depicted with golden breasts. The current church, built in the 1770s, stands at the head of a valley and there are dramatic views towards evening when the low sunlight emphasizes the relief of the land. The monks tend extensive vineyards below the monastery and produce and sell very palatable wines.

Agia Moni, about 2km (1 mile) from Chrysorrogiatissa, stands on the site of a temple dedicated to Hera, wife of Zeus. Abandoned in 1571, it has recently been renovated.

Panagia ★

Panagia, birthplace of Archbishop Makarios, is 3km (2 miles) northeast of Chrysorrogiatissa.

If you have time and enjoy driving this is country in which to wander. Be warned that with the smaller villages the way in is easy to find, the way out may not be the most obvious. One route to the village from Polis, via Simou, Lasa and Thrinia, offers spectacular panoramas and is well signposted. Maps suggest an alternative route via Peristerona and Filousa to the deserted Turkish villages of Sarama and Anadiou: four-wheel drive is essential.

TILLIRIA

Once famed for its copper deposits, Tilliria is a vast area of wooded conical peaks to the east of the Polis–Pafos road. This wild area falls within the **Pafos Forest** and an extensive network of well-maintained forest roads offers endless opportunities for those who need to escape the crowds. With care, four-wheel drive is not essential.

East of Koilineia the road deteriorates to a track at Vretsia and then descends to the upper end of the **Xeros Valley**. Here, the **Roudia Bridge**, now restored, formed part of the **Venetian camel route** established to carry copper ore from mines on the heights of Troödos to the sea coast at Pafos. In spring and early summer there is still an appreciable amount of water in the Xeros though in summer it lives up to its name (*xeros* means dry).

The geology of the area is remarkable: the road back to Pafos down the Diarizos Valley passes a succession of different coloured rocky outcrops where upheavals in the earth's crust have revealed long-hidden strata. The Turkish village of **Mamonia** has given its name to a series of ancient fossil-bearing rocks, the Mamonia Complex.

THE LAST COPPER MINE

Long before the 'golden' age, the rich copper deposits of the region were known throughout the area of the Mediterranean. Mining continued until the Limni Mine closed in 1979, when it became uneconomical since ore deposits of quality had become exhausted.

Opposite: *Panagia Chrysorrogatissa (Our Lady of the Golden Pomegranates) is still a working monastery, producing its own wines from vineyards tended by monks in the valley below.*
Left: *Remains of ancient aqueduct systems occur in the Xeros and other valleys.*

Right: *Where the Tillirian*
Troödos plunges to the sea
lies a coast of red-brown
cliffs and dark rocks: Kato
Pyrgos is about as far by
road as you can get from
Lefkosia yet only 60km
(37 miles) on the map.

WALKING THE CAMEL TRAIL

Venetian engineers built a
series of elegant bridges to
cross the river valleys along
the route from the copper
mines of Troödos: at Roudia,
Kelefos (across the Diarizos)
and Elaia. For a walker to
encompass all three bridges
in only a single day demands
considerable pre-planning.
However, the Xeros Valley
can also be reached from
Agios Nikolaos (see p. 57):
the road is 'jeepable' but it
is almost an insult to this
unspoiled area to attempt
to explore other than on foot.
Walking offers your best
chance of seeing Egyptian
vultures soaring high over the
terrain from the inaccessible
cliffs on which they nest. The
Kelefos bridge is approached
by a track running north from
Agios Nikolaos.

Cedar Valley ★★

Most visitors to the Tillirian Tröodos search for the Cedar
Valley, advertised widely in brochures but never crowded
as many give up before reaching it. It lies at the foot of
Mount Tripylos, on whose slopes grow the last natural
forests of indigenous cedar. The shortest route begins at
Panagia but for those with time (and determination) there
are longer routes via **Lysos** (southeast of Polis) or **Pomos** on
the north coast which are scenically rewarding.

Stavros tis Psokas ★

At the Government Forestry Station here there is a campsite, but it is also possible to
stay overnight in the balconied colonial buildings (booking is essential from June to
September). In the peaceful depths of the forest you can fall asleep lulled by the
mesmeric 'poop' sound of the scops owl and wake to the rustle and scent of pines.

From Stavros tis Psokas there are two well-marked nature trails and a chance for
the energetic to climb **Mount Tripylos** – at 1362m (4469ft) the highest peak in the
vicinity – or **Zacharou**, 1212m (3976ft).

Kato Pyrgos ★★

From Polis the coast road runs northeast past extensive fruit plantations – development is beginning here but it is still a far cry from that on the south coast. **Pomos** is the largest village but it has little to commend it except for a few tavernas and some self-catering apartments. Beyond the village lies dramatic coastal scenery where the road hugs the dark cliffs as the foothills of the Troödos tumble down into the sea.

The tortuous route through the hills circumnavigates the Turkish enclave of **Kokkina** to bring the determined driver back again to the coast road leading to Kato Pyrgos. Only UN troops can pass through the Greek and then Turkish checkpoints. Surprisingly, **Kato Pyrgos** is well-equipped with three hotels and it has an attractive beach. The Byzantine church of **Panagia Galoktisti** can be reached by walking up the valley towards Kaleri. Kato Pyrgos is about as far as you can get by road from Nicosia, thanks to the division of the island, but for an energetic crow it is only about 60km (37 miles) away.

At several points along the coast road from Polis signs suggest routes to Stavros tis Psokas (see p. 44). Distances might not look great on a map but the innumerable bends make the journey seem endless on a hot day. One road to Stavros begins from Pomos and follows the Livadi, an impressive torrent in spring and winter.

> ### MOUFLON EMBLEM OF CYPRUS
>
> The shy and agile mouflon – used by Cyprus Airways as its logo – is seldom seen in the wild. At Stavros a small captive breeding herd is kept penned. The Pafos Forest is the strong-hold of this wild sheep, whose exact origins are not known. Remains of these animals have been found in Neolithic settlements dating from 6000BC, when they may well have been domesticated. A survey in 1878, the first year of British rule, found only 20 animals. Numbers rose from 1939 when the Pafos Forest became a reserve and goat grazing was banned, removing competition for food. Mating takes place in November and both sexes grow a winter fleece of thick brown hair.

> ### THE CYPRUS CEDAR
>
> The Cyprus Cedar is related to the Cedar of Lebanon but has much shorter needles and is considered to be unique to the island. Pit props found in ancient copper mines show that it must once have occurred throughout the Troödos. Sadly, successive invaders exploited the island's timber reserves and the cedars were an inevitable casualty. The Forestry Department has now replanted extensive areas with these trees.

Left: *The endemic Cyprus cedar* (Cedrus libani *ssp.* brevifolia).

Akamas takes its name from the son of the Greek hero Theseus, and his link with the area is a romantic one. For it was here, according to legend, that he surprised the goddess Aphrodite revealed in all her unclad beauty (at the Baths of Aphrodite, naturally). She fell for him but the tryst was doomed from the outset because she was already married to the lame Hephaisitos, the blacksmith god. Akamas put the experience behind him and, so it is said, went on to found the ancient city kingdom of Soli.

Below: *Isolated and, as yet, unspoiled, Akamas attracts discerning visitors: from humans in search of its unique plants and a wild landscape for turtles burying their eggs on its beaches.*

Akamas ★★★

Proposed as the island's first **National Park** in 1989, Akamas embraces a total of 155km² (60 sq miles), encompassing a very varied terrain with beaches, cliffs, gorges and forests as well as a number of picturesque villages. The region's main feature is a rugged peninsula ending in **Cape Arnaoutis** (Cape Akamas), Cyprus' westernmost point with the tiny islet of Mazaki beyond. The northern side of this peninsula is comparatively lush while in the drier west there is extensive, almost impenetrable scrub where the island's few **foxes** still survive. The region's future is still far from secure; though the Friends of Akamas remain vigilant they were unable to prevent laws being changed to allow a hotel to be built within the park.

Nature in Akamas

The isolated, unspoiled area of Akamas supports a wealth of rare plants, the Cyprus tulip (*Tulipa cypria*) and orchids such as the very rare *Orchis punctulata* and small insect mimics (*Ophrys*) among them. Some plants have evolved over the millennia during which this area has been isolated to become quite distinct species endemic to the region. Several plants restricted to Akamas show this in their scientific names, such as the yellow-flowered Akamas Alyssum (*Alyssum akamassicum*) and a member of the thistle family, the pink Akamas Centaury (*Centaurea akamantis*).

The sandy beaches at **Lara** attract both green and loggerhead **turtles** which haul themselves laboriously ashore from late May into August to lay their eggs – reputedly on moonlit nights. Aware that large numbers of tourists and nesting sites for these animals do not mix, the conservation-minded Fisheries Department has waged a determined battle against development. Nests are located and the eggs, buried deep in the sand, are protected by a wire cage. The hatchlings are removed by patrols and taken to the sea in the evening safe from wandering foxes, their main predators. Empty eggshells, like broken ping-pong balls, can sometimes be found along the beach.

Exploring Akamas

The mountains along the peninsular spine end in a 'table top' rising to **Mavri Shinia** at 480m (1575ft) which can be reached wholly on foot by the energetic via a well-marked trail from **Loutra Aphroditis**. Views are stupendous: the land drops away in precipitous cliffs over tiny bays and inlets set in an azure sea. Alternatively, the heights can be gained via the village of **Neo Chorio**, where rooms are available for rent. A dirt road beyond the village leads to a roadside spring at **Smigies** and the tiny chapel of **Agios Minas**. Where the open pinewoods begin there is a picnic place complete with tables and cooking areas. Beyond, the dirt road divides – the left fork is negotiable with four-wheel drive, slowly and carefully without! The descent via hairpin bends offers breathtaking vistas of the sea and the road eventually reaches Lara Beach. The right fork leads to a forest road winding along the ridge to **Kefalovrisia** and an ancient site, **Kastroiotis Rigaenas,** where another picnic spot has been set up near a spring running beneath the shade of huge oak trees (often a feature of Lusignan settlements). In summer, try to make the final climb to the exposed heights in the early morning or evening, when the air is cooler.

Right: *Four-wheel drive vehicles are ideal for exploring, but increased numbers could threaten the environment.*

AKAMAS NATURE TRAILS

The **Baths of Aphrodite** are the starting-point for several nature trails. The CTO and the Cyprus Forestry Department have taken a lot of trouble to waymark paths on Akamas. Along the trails some of the plants are labelled with Greek (and Latin) numbers corresponding to leaflets which are available from the tourist office; they also provide a very good, free map of the area on a scale of 1:100,000. Be aware that the trails can turn into mud baths when it rains.

Loutra Aphroditis ★

Near the coast lies the spring known as the '**Baths of Aphrodite**', marked on every map but more remarkable for being permanently wet on a dry island than for living up to its romantic name. From here the coastal path leads to **Fontana Amorosa**, again exciting by name, disappointing in reality, being little more than a trickle in a cultivated area.

But the **cliff path** itself, scenically dramatic at any time, is spectacular in February and March when a profusion of pink and white cyclamen cascades towards the sea. In October the cooler air brings warm clear days for walking. The road, often in bad condition after winter rains, can be dangerous even in a four-wheel drive vehicle.

The Laona Project

This enterprise, set up by Cyprus Friends of the Earth and supported by the EC and the Leventis Foundation, offers grants to persuade villagers to avoid the mistakes of thoughtless development evident in Agia Napa and to attract the 'right kind' of tourists – in other words those in tune with the countryside and village life. Travellers in search of an escape from coastal tourist traps can now find renovated stone-built village houses in Ineia, Drouseia, Kritou Tera and Arodes perched high above the sea with commanding views and friendly neighbours (*see p. 50*).

Left: *High on the spine of Akamas, Drouseia commands extensive views over a patchwork of orchards, vineyards and deep gorges.*
Opposite top: *The Baths of Aphrodite.*
Opposite bottom: *Drifts of wild cyclamen* (Cyclamen persicum) *flower in kamas in early spring.*

Drouseia *

Loyal expatriates, many of them from Australia, annually swelled Drouseia's resident population. To cope with this influx a share-subscription resulted in the building of the Drouseia Heights Hotel, with commanding views north and west over Polis and Akamas and, to the east, where the Tillirian Troödos reaches the sea, mountains silhouetted dramatically in the dawn light. The village is delightful with its ancient stone houses; hotel guests can make arrangements to visit them through the manager.

This is an ideal centre for exploring parts of the region on foot. The attractive Byzantine church of **Agia Akaterini**, remarkable for its single dome and series of well-preserved arches, can be reached from the main road or from Drouseia through the village of Kritou Tera and then on a track running roughly northeast, which eventually descends to the 'river', Argaki tis Kampouras, and the main Pafos–Polis road. From Drouseia, donkey roads lead to **Fasli** and **Androlikou**, formerly Turkish villages but now deserted except for a single family and a multitude of goats. The deep gorge below Androlikou once housed a large colony of fruit bats but due to persecution by hunters they have moved elsewhere. There are paths from both Drouseia and Ineia to the craggy outcrop of **Agios Georgios**, at 668m (2192ft) the highest point in Akamas.

WHAT'S IN A NAME?

Villages in this region often have names which offer clues to those who originally settled there. The twin communities of Kato (lower) and Pano (upper) Arodes were established during the feudal rule of the Knights Hospitaller and named in honour of Rhodes, the main centre of the Order.

Tera and Kritou Tera trace their origins back to the Roman occupation, while Drouseia's original inhabitants came from Arcadia in the Peloponnese. Today, the Pafiot Greek dialect is distinctive, employing numerous words which have changed little since Homeric times: locals proudly boast that theirs is the 'true' Greek (a distinct version of Turkish was also used which shared many words with Greek). Drouseia, a local word for cool or fresh, is certainly apt for the hilltop village; alternatively, it could be a corruption of *dhrys*, the word for oak, which both fossil and archaeological evidence show once formed forests in the lowlands.

Pafos and the West at a Glance

Pafos Airport can become hopelessly overloaded – expect delays, limited facilities and considerable discomfort in summer. There is no public **bus** service but all charter operators provide transfer – **car hire** is available at the airport.

Intercity buses connect Pafos with Lemesos, Larnaca and Lefkosia and are operated by **Nea Amoroza**, tel: (26) 936822 or (26) 936740 and **Alepa Bus**, tel: (26) 934410. **Rural buses** to villages around Pafos, including Polis, operate from the Kara- vella Bus Station in the Mesogi Industrial area on the outskirts of town, tel: (26) 934252. Shared interurban service **taxis** with 4–8 seats operate every half hour between Pafos and Lemesos (06:00–18:00). Seats can be booked by phone and drivers pick up and drop off at any point within the city limits. Intercity taxis are operated by Pagkypria Eteria Yperastikon Taxi (Cyprus Interurban Taxis). For reservations from Pafos, tel: (26) 233181, 777474. **Solis Minibus**, tel: (22) 666388, for Polis-Pafos-Lemesos services. **Car-rental agencies: A Petsas & Sons**, Leoforos Apostolou Pavlou 86, Green Crt, tel: (26) 235522; **Andy Spyrou Rentals Ltd**, Leoforos Posidonos, Natalia Crt 19 and 20, Kato Pafos, tel: (26) 822633, and also at Pafos Airport, tel: (26) 422711; **Astra Self Drive**, Leoforos Apostolou Pavlou,

Marina Crt, tel: (26) 242252; **Hertz**, Leoforos Apostolou Pavlou 54A, tel: (26) 933985, fax: (26) 251163; **Fontana**, MPN Tourist Enterprises, PO Box 66244, Polis 8031, tel: (26) 32 3422 fax: (26) 321229.

In season most hotels are part of the package scene; CTO can help with vacancies. **Rooms** can be rented in Pafos and Polis.

Pafos
LUXURY

Elysium, Queen Verenikis St, Pafos, tel: (26) 844444, fax: (26) 844333, www.elysium.com.cy Opened in 2002, it may have been inspired by a monastery, but there is nothing monastic about this palatial retreat over- looking the Tombs of the Kings and the Mediterranean. Myriad restaurants, a huge outdoor pool and a poolside hot tub.
St George Hotel, Chlorakas, tel: (26) 845000, fax: (26) 845800, www.stgeorge-hotel.com 6km (4 miles) north of Pafos. Virtu- ally on the beach; great facili- ties for exercise lovers; priority facilities at Tsada Golf Club.

MID-RANGE

Dionysos, PO Box: 60141, tel: (26) 933414, fax: (26) 933908. Efficient, friendly, comfortable; great bar tastefully built to look like the antiquities of Pafos. **Axiothea**, PO Box 70, 2 Ivi Maliotii St, tel: (26) 932866, fax: (26) 945790. Friendly, reliable and well-run with good views over Nea Pafos.

Park Mansions, 16 Odos Pavlou Melas, Ktima, tel: (26) 945645. Delightful old Venetian-style mansion.

BUDGET

Kinyras, 91 Archbishop Makarios St, tel: (26) 941604. Stylish and affordable guest- house in old stone building; very attractive inner courtyard; good restaurant; just off the main square at Ktima Pafos.

Coral Bay
LUXURY

Leptos Coral Beach, Pegeia, tel: (26) 62 1601, fax: (26) 621156. Luxury self-contained resort with sandy beach, spa, pools, and children's facilities.

Polis
LUXURY

Anassa, Polis, tel: (26) 888000, anassa@thanos-hotel.com www.thanoshotels.com 5km south of Polis on the edge of the Akamas; lavish hotel; one of the best in Cyprus; private beach, superb views.

MID-RANGE

Droushia Heights, tel: (26) 332351, fax: (26) 332353. Wonderful views. Friendly, efficient and comfortable. **Marion**, PO Box 29, tel: (26) 321216, fax: (26) 321459. Clean, comfortable; legendary service at languid 'Polis' speed.

BUDGET

Guesthouse Trianon, 99 Makarios, Ktima Pafos, tel: (26) 232193. Pleasant, well

Pafos and the West at a Glance

managed guesthouse; 11 double and twin rooms, air-conditioning on request.

SELF-CATERING
Andreas Tavros, PO Box 199, Neo Chorio, tel: (26) 322421, fax: (26) 322496. Very well-appointed apartments near sea. Good for exploring Akamas.

VILLAGE HOUSES
Houses in Arodes, Akourdaleia, Drouseia, Kritou Tera and other villages can be rented via the **Laona Project** in Akamas: **Sunvil Holidays**, Sunvil House, 7 and 8 Upper Square, Old Isleworth, TW7 7BJ, tel: (0208) 568 4499, fax: (0208) 568 8330, www.sunvil.co.uk Contact Artemis Yiordamlis, Laona Project, PO Box 257, Lemesos.

FOREST STATION
Stavros tis Psokas in Pafos Forest: beds bookable in advance, tel: (26) 722338.

CAMPING
Feggari Camping, Coral Bay, Pegeia, tel: (26) 621534. **Polis Camping Site**, tel: (26) 321526. 200 tents. In eucalyptus grove near beach and town.

WHERE TO EAT
Pafos
Fish tavernas at the harbour produce meals of good standard. Fish is locally caught (but squid is probably from Taiwan). **Chez Alex**, 7 Constantia St, tel: (26) 234767. Not on the seafront, but the fish is fresher. Menu depends on the catch.

Loukoudi, 6 Market St, tel: (26) 245893. In the market arcade – seasonal menu, local specialities and fresh pastries. **Nicos Tyrimos Fish Taverna**, 71 Agapinoros St, tel: (26) 942846. A town restaurant that locals will choose to dine in. The owner has his own fishing boat so the food tends to be fresher. **Seven St Georges Tavern**, Yeroskepos, tel: (09) 9655824, www.7stgeorgestavern.com Owner George Yeroskepos spends the evening working the tables with a huge smile and plenty of tall stories. The taverna uses as much homegrown organic vegetables in its expansive meze meals as possible.

North and West
Agios Georgios, Pegeia, tel: (26) 621306. Traditional taverna; overlooks bay; fresh fish. **Panicos Corallo Restaurant**, Coral Bay, Pegeia, tel: (26) 62 1052. International cuisine using high quality ingredients. **Pithary Tavern**, Kissonerga, tel: (26) 241357. A favourite with locals; international menu.

Porto Latchi
Porto Latchi, tel: (26) 321529, www.portolatchi.com The

interior of the old carob mill is the liveliest dining space.

East
Leda Village Tavern, Kouklia, tel: (26) 432059. Traditional Cypriot food. **Old Country Tavern**, Nikoklia, tel: (26) 432211. On the road to Troödos via Agios Nikolaos. Lovely old stone building; traditional Cypriot cooking. Some rooms for an overnight stay.

TOURS AND EXCURSIONS
Travel agents offer **coach tours** (details in hotel foyers). **Boat trips** from Pafos harbour, Lakki and Coral Bay (Agios Georgios). 'Safari' operators offer **treks** (some more interested in picnics than wildlife) – try **Exalt**, PO Box 337, Pafos or Agias Kyriakis 24, Kato Pafos, tel: (26) 143803.

USEFUL CONTACTS
Cyprus Tourism Organisation, Odos Gladstonos 3, CY 8046 Ktima Pafos, tel: (26) 932841, and in lower Pafos at Poseidonos 63, tel: (26) 930521. **Pafos General Hospital**, tel: (26) 241111. **Polis Hospital**, tel: (26) 321431.

PAFOS	J	F	M	A	M	J	J	A	S	O	N	D
AVERAGE TEMP. °C	13	13	15	16	19	23	24	25	23	20	17	13
AVERAGE TEMP. °F	55	55	59	61	66	73	75	77	73	68	63	55
HOURS OF SUN DAILY	6	6	6	8	10	11	11	11	9	7	6	5
RAINFALL mm	150	150	150	200	125	–	–	–	75	125	150	175
RAINFALL in	6	6	6	8	5	–	–	–	3	5	6	7
DAYS OF RAINFALL	7	6	6	6	3	–	–	–	5	6	6	7

3
Troödos

Forming the island's mountainous backbone, the peaks of the Troödos culminate in Mount Olympus, a great whale-back of a mountain composed of volcanic rock which rises to 1952m (6404ft) at **Chionistra**. The name means 'snow-pit' and snow was gathered here in Ottoman times to be taken to Nicosia. The heights are snow-covered from January until March and have become a venue for skiers, easily reached from Lemesos so that it is possible to swim in the morning and ski in the afternoon.

In high summer the Troödos offers a cool escape from the lowlands. Virtually from the inception of British rule the administrators moved up here, lock, stock, families and filing systems, to escape the heat. They erected their houses in colonial style with verandahs, reminiscent of Indian hill stations, and for recreation they walked, creating a series of easy contour paths from which to enjoy the stunning views.

Strictly, the term 'Troödos' refers to the heights within a radius of 4–5km (3 miles) of the Troödos resort, but it is often taken to encompass the whole massif. To appreciate the region's extent take a walk on the **Artemis trail** (*see p. 54*) around Chionistra: rows of forested peaks unfold endlessly to the west and in early spring the distant valleys are dressed in a haze of white when the cherry, peach and apple trees are in bloom.

In addition to its natural beauty, Troödos is the setting for a remarkable group of lavishly frescoed Byzantine churches dating from the 11th to the 16th centuries.

TURKEY

CYPRUS   • Lefkosia
         (Nicosia)
Troödos •

MEDITERRANEAN SEA

DON'T MISS

*** Madari Ridge Trail: incredible views.
*** Fikardou: the beautifully restored village.
*** Machairas Monastery: in its dramatic setting.
*** Frescoes: in the tiny church at **Asinou** and in **Agios Nikolaos tis Stegis**.
** Troödos: walking trails.
** Caledonia Falls: at the end of the Caledonia Trail.
** Kakopetria and **Galata:** mountain villages.

Opposite: *Pedoulas and Moutoullas in the Marathasa Valley.*

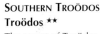

SKIING

Skiing in Cyprus is great fun for islanders or visitors including it in a general holiday, but not for those hoping to discover new ski destinations. The season runs from January to March, occasionally longer. Equipment can be hired in Sun Valley where there are four short runs of about 200m each (tuition is available). The north face has longer, more difficult descents and there are two tracks (4km and 8km) for cross-country. The slopes tend to be crowded at weekends; competitions are held on the north face.

Below: *The tradition of icon painting is preserved at Troöditissa where monks still live in the monastery high in the Troödos mountains, surrounded by pines and well-tended orchards.*

SOUTHERN TROÖDOS
Troödos ★★

The resort of Troödos – village is not quite the right term for its cluster of restaurants and gift shops – provides meals and hot drinks in winter for skiers and *souvlakia*, *sheftalia* and salads for large numbers of Cypriot families in summer. Four trails – known as **Artemis**, **Atalanta**, **Caledonia** and **Persephone** – have been carefully laid out and labelled by the Forestry Department in conjunction with the CTO: a detailed brochure giving maps of the routes and a key to the unique rocks, plants and points of interest en route is available from CTO offices. On a clear day the vistas are staggering: the salt lake at Akrotiri looks Lilliputian, the forests to the west seem endless and far beyond the plain to the north lie the snow-capped Taurus mountains of southern Turkey.

Prodromos ★

After British rule ended, Prodromos, once a colonial hill resort, attracted a new, wealthy clientele from Egypt, Lebanon and Israel: some owned villas while others stayed in the now-closed Hotel Berengaria, a venerable preserve of genteel service and old-world manners, which was abandoned in 1980.

Prodromos competes with **Pano Amiantos** for the title of highest hill village in Cyprus at 1400m (4600ft). It is located on the 'scenic' route which ascends Troödos up the **Marathasa Valley**. From Prodromos the shortest route to Troödos ascends the north face, past the ski lifts; the longer route to the south goes first to **Platres**, another hill resort and still a popular base for visitors to the Troödos.

Trooditissa ★

The present buildings o...
1200m (3950ft) up in the m...
It was founded in the 13th...
resting-place for a miraculous i...
from Asia Minor in the 8th centur...
hermits in a cave and then found, c...
deaths, revealed by its preternat...
monastery is also home to a metal gird...
induce fertility in any female who puts it o...

Foini ★

Foini is most easily reached by car from Platr...
Mandria) – there is also a road from Prodromos, ma...
a round trip quite possible. The attractive work...
village lies well away from the main tourist routes.
Foini has a reputation for its skilled potters who made
the huge clay storage jars (*pithari*) which were produced
in situ. The **Folk Art Museum** of Theophanis Pivlakis,
established in his traditional village house, includes
details of how they were made.

Foini is the place to buy local delicacies: *louk-oumades*, *soutsoukou* and fiery *zivania*.

TROÖDOS

Platres ★ ... for ... in summ...

A HIGHLAND RETREAT

The summer residence of the president is sited in the woods near ... dating from 1890 the ... British High C... ... the buildi...

... woods near
...mos become a sea
... deep pink when masses of
paeonies come into flower:
they may have been intro-
duced by monks who grew
them for medicinal purposes.

Other plants in flower in
the same season include
Lusitanian milk vetch and
purple rock cress.

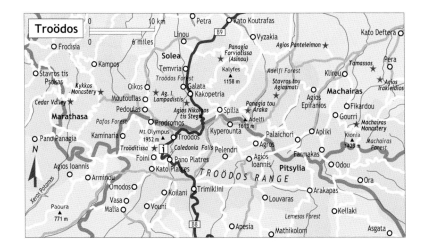

Pano Platres becomes a busy place of escape ...eople fleeing the energy-sapping heat of the towns. There is little sign now of the exclusivity that once made Platres and nearby Prodromos hill resorts for the wealthy. But the equable local climate persists, enhanced by the Kryos River and the pine forests where nightingales, in spite of their reputation, sing by day as well as late into the night. Spring and autumn are the best times to visit for those who wish to use Platres as a base for **walking** (or mountain biking) or just to escape the crowds: out of the high season there is ample space in the modest hotels.

...the ...mmissioner. ...g work was ...vised by a 26-year-old Frenchman who was later to achieve fame as a poet – Arthur Rimbaud.

Kato Platres lies some distance to the southwest of Pano Platres. There are fruit trees all round the village and in season the produce is sold from roadside stalls. Just south of the village the soil changes suddenly from volcanic brown to white chalk, and vine-growing becomes the major agricultural activity.

Omodos ★

The villages of this area have become known as the **Krassochorio** (literally, 'wine villages'), where on hillsides criss-crossed by endless ancient stone walls vines grow on the dry soils. The bulk of the crop is used to produce full-bodied red wines. In late summer, ancient overladen lorries, groaning under their burden, descend towards the coastal wineries. Esoteric road signs state, 'Beware, roads slippery with grape juice.'

Omodos, once a delightful hill village approached in spring along a scenic avenue of blossoming cherry trees, has now become a much-hyped tourist attraction. Its

appeal is still evident, however, even if the hard-headed realism of the tourist industry contrasts quite strongly with the natural Cypriot hospitality: if you want the donkey man in your picture, you

Left: *Southern Troödos is dotted with wineries, several of which offer the visitor free wine tasting.*

pay. The village is built around the **Monastery of Timiou Stavrou** (which has an unusual cane ceiling) sitting in a large cobbled square.

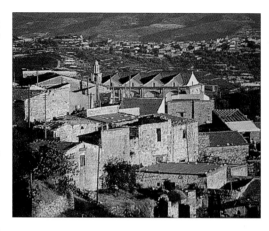

Vasa ★★

Built above a deep gorge, Vasa is one of a number of old villages dating back to Lusignan times. In contrast to Omodos it has managed to preserve its ancient charm. Village houses in crumbling disrepair just a few years ago have now been carefully renovated, and you can glimpse courtyards hidden behind stone walls and rooms divided by ancient arches. The taverna serves authentic Cypriot dishes and an excellent home-produced wine. **Potamiou** and **Vouni** to the east of Vasa have also been listed for protection. To the north, **Koilani** is the home of working artists and has an **Ecclesiastical Museum**. Further up the Kryos Gorge is the 12th-century chapel of **Agia Mavri**.

The surrounding countryside must rank as some of the most impressive in the island: narrow roads snake across hillsides and down into deeply incised valleys.

Although the land has been worked for centuries it retains a wild, empty feel. Signposts near **Malia** suggest two routes to Pafos: one via a fast new road, the other via **Arsos**, **Agios Nikolaos**, **Arminou** and **Salamiou**. Take the latter if you have time: the roads are narrow but metalled, the landscape unforgettable. A detour to Agios Ioannis brings you high above the **Xeros Gorge** (see p. 43). Two other routes to the south coast from Malia run via the parallel valleys of the **Diarizos** and the **Chapotami** – take them in the early morning or towards evening, when the low sun sculpts the hills.

Above: *An ancient unspoiled village in a dry chalk landscape, Vouni, partly deserted, lies in an area with a long tradition of wine-making.*

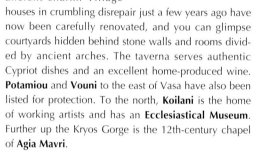

TROÖDOS SPECIALS

In spite of the rigours of the climate, from baking summers with frequent thunderstorms to snow-covered winters, Troödos is a botanical treasure house. Of the island's 127 endemic species of flowering plants 67 are unique to this area: many have 'troodii' as part of their Latin name. They include *Crocus cyprius*, which flowers as the snow melts on the heights, low-growing bushes of the Troödos Golden Drop (*Onosma troodii*), a unique wild garlic (*Allium troodii*), the yellow *Alyssum troodii* and the Troödos Mint (*Nepeta troodii*).

SOLEA

This northern region of Troödos around the Karyotis River valley is studded with **Byzantine churches**. Most of these small Orthodox churches began as simple rectangles to which a dome and entrance hall (narthex) were later added. Many were subsequently given steeply pitched roofs to protect the domes from heavy winter snowfalls. Hidden away in the mountains, they retained their wall paintings throughout the Ottoman period, leaving a fine legacy of Byzantine art. Most of the paintings illustrate scenes from the New Testament, and the frescoes fall into several different periods; the oldest are by artists from Syria and Cappadocia.

Kakopetria ★

Only in recent years has Kakopetria caught the imagination of developers, who have constructed houses along the sides of the wooded Solea Valley: buildings in the centre of the town have been restored and are protected by law. It is very much a summer resort, popular with Cypriots – especially on Sundays – with cafés, small hotels and several restaurants which are deservedly well-known for their locally caught trout.

Agios Nikolaos tis Stegis ★★★

The church of 'St Nicholas of the Roof' lies some 3km (2 miles) from Kakopetria up the valley of the Karyotis. Its name refers to its large pitched roof which hides the 11th-century dome beneath. The church contains many fine frescoes dating from the 11th to the 17th centuries: the 14th-century *Nativity* is particularly impressive.

> ### THE LEGEND OF KAKOPETRIA
>
> The village name means 'bad stone' – a reference to a boulder which reputedly stood on the hillside. Newly-weds would walk up to the stone which was credited with bringing them good luck. On one unlucky occasion, however, it rolled over spontaneously and crushed the hapless couple beneath.

It is possible (preferably with a four-wheel drive vehicle) to take the forest road fording the stream where the road descends to the trout farm: eventually this track meets up with the main road situated just below Platania. Walkers can scramble up the river bed (though this is almost impossible to do during the winter months) to a series of low **waterfalls**. Instead of returning to Kakopetria from Agios Nikolaos, enterprising drivers can take an alternative and much more exciting route to the heights of Troödos, following forestry roads along the north shoulder, with unbeatable views back over the Solea Valley.

Galata ★★

Down the valley from Kakopetria, its fertile terrain fed by numerous springs, Galata boasts four Byzantine churches. The two containing the most noteworthy paintings both date from the 16th century and are adjacent: **Michail Archangelos** (also known as Panagia Theotokos) has frescoes painted in 1514 by Symeon Axenti, a Cypriot artist, while those of **Panagia Podythou**, built in 1502, show a Venetian influence.

Asinou Church ★★★

The finest of all the painted churches in the island, **Panagia Forviotissa** is better known as Asinou after a long-disappeared Greek settlement. This tiny church stands on a bare hilltop surrounded by woods, with a river just beyond. The church dates from 1105 – the dome and narthex were added in 1200 – and the frescoes are almost a catalogue of Byzantine art. Five layers of paintings span the period from the building of the church to the 16th century. A booklet is available which explains both the history of the frescoes and their thematic designs.

TROÖDOS CHURCHES

The churches on UNESCO's list represent the cream: Asinou, Agios Ioannis Lampadistis, Agios Nikolaos tis Steyis, Panagia tou Araka and Stavros tou Agiasmati. Occasionally, you may find the church already open for other visitors. To find the caretaker ask in the nearest village café. Don't expect a guided tour with a discussion of the finer points of Byzantine art, but using a little Greek helps – it's amazing what can be conveyed with willingness and a smile. There are no admission charges, but a suitable donation is CY£1.00.

Opposite: *Kakopetria is a popular summer resort for holidaying Cypriots – out of season it is ideally placed for exploring the Troödos area.*
Left: *The tiny church of Asinou is generally held to be the finest of the island's many painted churches.*

Above: *Reputedly wealthy beyond the dreams of avarice, Kykkos monastery controls extensive land-holdings.*
Opposite: *Part of the church's altar screen.*

MARATHASA

The Marathasa Valley, drained by the **Setrachos** River, is deep and canyon-like. Although it runs parallel to the Solea Valley – separated from it by a high ridge – its villages are not nearly as dedicated to the tourist trade.

Pedoulas occupies a commanding position at the head of the Marathasa Valley and is a good base from which to explore the region. The 15th-century frescoed church of **Michail Archangelos** is on a side street in the lower part of the village.

Moutoullas ★

Your first encounter with the name Moutoullas is likely to be on the label of a bottle of natural mineral water: the restorative quality of the local spring water (bottled down in the valley) is responsible for a flourishing trade. Moutoullas has always thrived on the reputation of its craftsmen: they still make wooden implements for bread-making from pine – *sanidhes* or 'sandalwood'. These long planks with up to 11 hollows, used for proving the dough, are attractive but would be difficult to take home as souvenirs: more portable are the semi-cylindrical bowls called *vournes*. The tiny church of **Panagia tou Moutoulla** stands at the highest point of the village: built in 1279, it is the oldest surviving gable-roofed church on the island.

Kalopanagiotis ★★

Communities have settled at Kalopanagiotis, high on the northern slopes, since pagan times, attracted by its three therapeutic **sulphur springs**. There are some very attractive old houses with tiled roofs in the village and several modest hotels cater for a steady, if not thriving, spa trade. At weekends the main draw is the lake formed by the nearby **dam**: a pleasant spot for both fishing and picnics.

No fewer than three churches (Agios Heracleides, Agios Lampadistis and a Latin chapel) nestle together under an enormous barn roof which covers the monastery of **Agios Ioannis Lampadistis**. The buildings, which have remained intact although now disused, are sited across the river from Kalopanagiotis and are reached along a track. The frescoes are remarkable, spanning the 13th to 15th centuries, and virtually all the stories from the synoptic gospels are illustrated. The churches are open every day except at siesta time.

Kykkos Monastery ★

Situated on a pine-covered ridge at the edge of the Tillirian Troödos, Kykkos has always played a rather prominent role in the Greek Orthodox church. It acquired immense wealth from its land in Cyprus (large areas of land in Lefkosia are owned by the church) as well as property it once owned in mainland Greece, Asia Minor and Russia.

At weekends the monastery is a place of **pilgrimage**, especially for conveyor-belt baptisms of babies, and there are guest rooms available for Cypriot visitors. In EOKA days the monastery played an important part in sheltering the guerrillas.

Throni, the hill about 2km (1 mile) from Kykkos, is the final resting-place of **Archbishop Makarios III** who entered the monastery at the age of 12 and rose to become its Abbot, before becoming President. From the shrine on the hill above his tomb there are incredible views to Mount Olympus to the east and over the vast emptiness of the Tillirian hills in the west.

GLYKA

Although much of the soft fruit of Troödos is sold fresh, Cypriot women are initiated by their mothers, aunts and grandmothers into the secrets of producing *glyka* (*reçel*): fruits marinated in syrup. Fortunately, these are widely available outside Cypriot homes – try *petrokerasi* (dark cherries), *kitromilo* (baby Seville oranges), *siko* (figs) and *vazanaki* (tiny aubergines stuffed with almonds).

Above: *High above the thriving Agros village stands a hotel built by the villagers.*

MAMAS: PATRON SAINT OF TAX-EVADERS

At Louvaras the chapel is dedicated to St Mamas, a devout Byzantine hermit and the subject of a somewhat allegorical miracle. Mamas was arrested by the local governor when he refused to pay income tax – after all, he survived on alms on which tax had, presumably, already been paid. As he was being dragged off a lion leapt onto a lamb grazing nearby: Mamas ordered the beast to desist, picked up the lamb and rode the lion into town... and thereafter paid no taxes. No lions have ever been seen on the island before or since. So Mamas became the much-worshipped patron saint of tax-evaders (and accountants).

PITSYLIA

This land of deep valleys and bare ridges, known for its fruit and nut-growing, has a total population of only 21,000 divided amongst its 49 villages, although the largest of these – **Agros**, **Kyperounta** and **Palaichori** – are more like small towns.

Remoteness attracted Greek Cypriot settlers fleeing the Ottoman invasion and, though the area had been populated for centuries, that same isolation meant that Pitsylia suffered from the exodus of its young people. In an attempt to reverse the region's fortunes, the government set up the Pitsylia Integrated Rural Development, backed by the World Bank. Irrigation schemes have been constructed, but what has really made the area viable is a series of new roads, enabling people to work in the offices of Lefkosia and Lemesos as well as growing fruit and vegetables commercially at weekends.

Agros is an ideal base from which to explore the region. This is a lovely working village which has a reputation for its ham, sausages and rose water. The impressive Rodon hotel dominates the ridge above Agros: built by share subscription from the inhabitants, it is an important part of the local economy.

Churches of Pitsylia

There are three frescoed churches lying towards the south of the main Troödos ridge. Two are in **Pelendri** to the southwest: one, the 14th-century church of **Stavros**, has a narrow high dome supported by four columns, and the other, **Panagia**, lies across the valley and has 16th-century frescoes and a 'barn roof'. In **Louvaras**, south of Agros, the tiny church of **Agios Mamas** dates from 1454 and houses a remarkable collection of paintings by master, Philip Goul. Another of Goul's churches – **Metamorfosi tou Sotirou** – is at **Palaichori**, where Pitsylia meets the Machairas forest.

The northern slopes of Pitsylia can be conveniently reached from Lefkosia. One route via the suburb of Strovolos allows detours into the **Machairas** area (*see p. 64*). Alternatively, by turning south off the main B9 Lefkosia–Troödos road at **Peristerona**, you can take the scenically exciting approach to Pitsylia via **Orounta**.

The road climbs to **Lagoudera** where the attraction is the church of **Panagia tou Araka**, with frescoes painted in 1192. In the next valley to the east is the delightful church of **Stavros tou Agiasmati**, all that now remains of a former monastery. You will need to approach it by a roundabout route via Platanistasa if you wish to obtain the key. Here, too, the frescoes are the work of Philip Goul.

The Madari Ridge ★★★

In spring and autumn Pitsylia offers a great deal to the walker. The **Madari Ridge nature trail** meanders along the boundary between Lemesos and Lefkosia districts, with commanding views on either side. The route is marked from **Kyperounta**, where a track leads up to the wooden arch at the start of the trail; alternatively start from **Chandria**. The summit of **Adelfi** can be reached from the ridge. **Papoutsa** is the peak lying further along to the southeast, most easily scaled from the Palaichori–Agios Theodoros road. There is a stone shelter and a large cross on the summit and the panorama is staggering.

Pitsylia has special attractions for botanists in spring, when some of the island's rarest bulbous plants flower briefly, and well away from prying eyes: **Hartmann's Crocus** and the delicate blue **Lady Lock's Chionodoxa.**

Below: *Lady Lock's chionodoxa (Chionodoxa lochiae) is one of the island's rarest plants.*

AFXENTIOU'S TOMB

Below the monastery of Machairas a path leads to the cave where Gregor Afxentiou, a prominent EOKA member (who had been sheltered by the monks) was eventually cornered. His colleagues surrendered but he did not – although wounded he determinedly held off a platoon of 60 British troops for ten hours: he was eventually killed by a petrol bomb thrown into the cave.

MACHAIRAS

The Machairas Forest takes its name from the 12th-century monastery to the north of Mount Kionia. The region offers an easy day's excursion from Nicosia, driving southwest from Strovolos towards Palaichori.

Fikardou ★★★

The road from **Klirou** leads through a landscape where in spring streams run in the gorges and a succession of blooms brightens the countryside: cherry blossom, scarlet poppies and yellow crown daisies are followed by wild lavender and pink and white rock roses.

Traditional hill villages exhibit a style of rural architecture which has almost vanished, using bricks made of sun-baked mud or dung mixed with straw, and with tiled roofs. **Fikardou** has been rescued from inevitable disrepair by the Museum Service, which is slowly restoring the buildings. The **houses of Achilleas Demitri and Katsinioros** are open to the public (09:00–13:00 and 14:00–16:00 daily). They date, in part, from the 16th century and contain typical traditional furniture and implements.

The road follows the **Akaki** River; beyond Gourri the attraction *en route* to Machairas is the tiny village of **Lazanias**, with its ancient tumble-down houses nestling on the hillside.

Machairas Monastery ★★

The monastery's foundation in 1148 began in time-honoured fashion with the discovery of a miraculous icon (painted by St Luke) by two hermits from Palestine. Funds were provided for the original construction by the Emperor Comnenos. The monastery had to

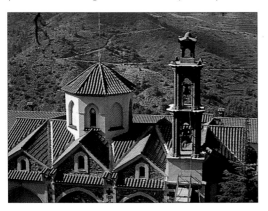

be rebuilt following two fires – in 1530 and 1892 – and is remarkable for its setting rather than its architecture.

The road to **Farmakas** passes a large dam built to flood the lower valley. On the northern face of the main Troödos ridge Farmakas and **Kampi** perch in commanding positions. On the south side lies the village of

Odou. In autumn plane trees in the valley below add a golden warmth to an already spectacular landscape. Numerous small roads take the traveller into the **Orini** region, an area virtually untouched by tourism.

Tamassos ★

Tamassos, occupied since 2500BC, was long famed as a centre of copper mining and export. By 800BC it was a Phoenician colony, but later mine owners included Alexander the Great and King Herod. In 1874 several tombs were excavated, possibly belonging to kings of Tamassos. The site is open 09:00–15:00 Tuesday–Friday, 10:00–15:00 weekends, closed Monday.

Agios Irakleidios ★

Tamassos was the birthplace of two of the island's saints: the first, Irakleidios, served as a guide to the apostles Paul and Barnabas on their visit to Cyprus and subsequently became the island's first bishop; his successor, Mnason, built up a reputation for his miracle-working.

The old monastery of **Agios Irakleidios**, destroyed and rebuilt several times since it was founded in the 4th century, was taken over by nuns in 1963. It is peaceful and charming, filled with plants carefully tended by the occupants: those living in Lefkosia get their pot plants here. Also on sale are honey and *kapari* (capers).

APOLLO'S HEAD

In 1836 a bronze statue of Apollo, cast in Athens in the 5th century, was discovered on the site of **Tamassos** by local farmers. Unfortunately, they broke it up and sold the valuable bronze to a scrap metal merchant. The head alone was salvaged and now resides in the British Museum.

Opposite: *The monastery of Machairas.*
Below: *Farmakas reservoir, popular with fishermen and picnickers.*

Troödos at a Glance

You can reach the Troödos region by road from Lefkosia, Lemesos and Pafos. Local buses offer local colour but are geared to the needs of villagers – they usually leave the village at around 07:00 or even earlier: **EAL**, tel: (25) 370592, operates interurban buses between Lemesos-Platres-Troödos Square and Troödos Sq-Platres-Lemesos (except on weekends and public holidays).

The best way to explore is by **car** to the villages and then on **foot**, or on the increasingly popular **mountain bike**, available for hire in Platres. **Rural taxis** are also available in all the larger villages.

Much of Troödos is largely off the tourist track once the coach trips leave at the end of the day. In summer the mountain resorts are very popular with Cypriots escaping the heat of the plains – in the winter months the hotels close through lack of custom (except those which serve skiers on Chionistra). In spring and autumn hotel or pension accommodation is easy to find on spec.

Troödos
Jubilee, tel: (25) 420107, fax: (22) 673391. One of a kind,

based around a series of chalets, the hotel is unpretentious and comfortable with good food. Superbly sited for walking. Activity holidays are available for children in the summer months. A good centre for skiers in winter when it also offers roaring fires.

BUDGET
Youth Hostel, tel: (25) 424400. Situated on the Troödos–Kakopetria road about 400m from the Troödos Square. Open Apr–Oct, weather permitting.

CAMPING
Troödos Hill Resort, tel: (25) 421624. Situated 2km downhill from the square, off the main Troödos–Kakopetria road, in a pine forest. Open May to end Oct, weather permitting.

Platres
LUXURY
Forest Park, tel: (25) 421751, fax: (25) 421875, website: www.forestpark hotel.com.cy Well-appointed luxury hotel surrounded by pine forests.

MID-RANGE
Pendeli, tel: (25) 421736, fax: (25) 421808, website: www.pendelihotel.com Comfortable, unpretentious and friendly.
Edelweiss, tel: (25) 421335, fax: (25) 422060. This small,

friendly and comfortable establishment offers very good value for money.

Agros
LUXURY
Rodon, tel: (25) 521201, fax: (25) 521235, website: www.swaypage.com/rodon Superbly situated on a ridge with commanding views. Built by share subscription from villagers and expatriates – efficient, comfortable, good traditional food and very friendly: management committed to encouraging eco-tourism. Ideal for walkers and exploring Pitsylia.
Vlachos, tel: (25) 521330, fax: (25) 521890. Located on the high street but remarkably cheap, clean and friendly. Offers an excellent buffet supper.

Kakopetria
MID-RANGE
Hellas, tel: (22) 922450, fax: (22) 922227. Small comfortable hotel, popular with Lefkosians.

BUDGET
Kifissia, tel: (22) 922421. On the road to Agios Nikolaos tis Stegis – good value.

Pedoulas
MID-RANGE
Churchill Pinewood Valley, tel: (22) 952211, fax: (22) 952439. This popular and

Troödos at a Glance

comfortable resort offers hotel accommodation as well as some self-catering apartments.

BUDGET

Marangos, tel: (22) 952657. This old stone building with panoramic views is situated on the road to Kykkos. It is comfortable and very good value, but is open only during July and August. **Christy's Palace**, tel: (22) 952655. On the main commercial street but cheap, very cheerful and open all year round.

Krassochorio

Vasa, tel: (25) 364718, fax: (25) 346333. Traditional village houses tastefully renovated in a very friendly village with coffee shop and bakery. Bookable through **Sunvil Holidays**, Sunvil House, 7 & 8 Upper Square, Old Isleworth, Middx TW7 7BJ, tel: (0208) 568 4499, fax: (0208) 568 8330, website: www.sunvil.co.uk

WHERE TO EAT

Roadside Tavernas in the Troödos are usually quite cheap and cheerful and all serve much the same basic fare: there are dips to start, accompanied by village bread, then a meat course (*sheftalia* or *kleftiko*) with village salad. In the valleys you can expect to find trout from the local farms.

Kakopetria

Maryland at the Mill, tel: (22) 922536. Noted for its local trout and spectacular setting on the banks of the river. The restaurant is best visited after the lunchtime and afternoon trippers have departed.

Platres

Kalidonia, tel: (25) 421404. An unpretentious and friendly family restaurant with good traditional cooking. Their *trachanas* soup is particularly welcome in cold weather.

Southern Troödos

Foini Tavern – Taste of Village, tel: (25) 421828. Unusually for a village restaurant, this one does not serve the predictable traditional fare. The restaurant is quite popular with those in the know who travel up from Lemesos (a 30-min drive).
Lania Taverna, tel: (25) 432398. On the outskirts of a picturesque hill village – very good traditional cooking: their specialities include vegetarian meals which are

prepared to order.
Vasa Village Taverna, tel: (25) 942185. Serves some of the best traditional food in Cyprus – including vegetarian dishes – with copious village wine.

TOURS AND EXCURSIONS

Day and half-day coach trips visit the Troödos region – especially the hill resorts – from the main tourist centres on the coast. A range of well-planned, highly scenic **mountain-bike routes**, graded from novice to difficult, is offered by the **Jubilee Mountain Bike Centre**, Jubilee Hotel, Troödos, tel: (25) 421547, fax: (25) 463991. Bikes can be hired on a daily or weekly basis at very reasonable rates.

USEFUL CONTACTS

Cyprus Ski Federation, Troödos, tel: (25) 420165 or (25) 420104/5.
Lefkosia General Hospital, tel: (22) 801400.
Kyperounta Hospital, tel: (25) 532021.
Tourist Office, Platres, tel: (25) 421316.

TROÖDOS	J	F	M	A	M	J	J	A	S	O	N	D
AVERAGE TEMP. °C	8	9	12	17	21	26	29	29	25	20	16	11
AVERAGE TEMP. °F	47	48	54	62	70	79	84	84	77	69	60	51
SUNSET	16.45	17.30	17.45	19.15	19.45	20.00	20.00	19.30	19.00	17.15	16.45	16.45
RAINFALL mm	250	200	160	80	–	–	–	–	–	–	80	250
RAINFALL in	10	8	6	3	–	–	–	–	–	–	3	10

4
Lemesos (Limassol) and the South

The importance of Lemesos (Limassol) to the Republic's economy surged following the Turkish invasion of 1974, when its population almost doubled with the arrival of 45,000 Greek Cypriot refugees. It is now the island's **second city** and most important **port** (for ferries and containers). Lemesos boasts the most tourist 'beds' in Cyprus, mainly in the long ribbon development of hotels, night clubs and restaurants stretching along the coast as far as **Amathus**, 13km (8 miles) to the east.

The main Lefkosia–Lemesos highway runs to the north of the city and is as near as many choose to get to the sprawling conurbation visible from its carriageways. However, in spite of modern development the city centre, with its old stone buildings, retains some charm. Bronze Age finds from 1300BC have revealed a coastal settlement – Nemesos or Lemesos – though it was dwarfed by Amathus to the east and **Kourion** to the west.

Many local industries are produce-related: canning, carob-milling, wine-making and the export of fruit and vegetables. Newer factories make designer-label clothing, bags and shoes. The fortunes of Lemesos were founded on growing – first **sugar cane**, followed by **citrus** – but those fortunes foundered after a series of serious earthquakes. The city was burned by the Genoese in 1371, raided by Arabs and finally sacked by the Ottoman Turks in 1539. Recovery only began in earnest with increased **wine exports** and the rebuilding of the **harbour** towards the end of the 19th century.

TURKEY

CYPRUS · Lefkosia (Nicosia)

· Lemesos (Limassol)

MEDITERRANEAN SEA

Don't Miss

*** Limassol Wine Festival: held in September.
*** Ancient Curium: impressive cliff-top theatre.
*** Petra tou Romiou: dazzling sunsets.
** Flamingos: at Akrotiri salt lake in winter and spring.
**Kolossi: a Crusader castle.

Opposite: *Imposing columns mark the site of a temple to an important Cypriot deity – Apollo Hylates, god of the woodland and protector of the city of Kourion.*

Above: *Little remains of Amathus to show its former glory and grand scale.*

The Citadel ★★

Now housing the **Cyprus Medieval Museum** (open Monday–Friday 07:30–17:00, Saturday 09:00–17:00, open until 18:00 in summer, closed Sunday), the citadel was built early in the 14th century on the site of the old Byzantine castle where Richard the Lion-heart married Berengaria in the chapel on 12 May 1191; here, too, Richard was crowned King of Cyprus and Berengaria Queen of England by the Bishop of Evreux. The present building was extensively renovated in 1950 (up to 1940 it was still being used as a prison by the colonial administration). Included in the collection is part of the **Lambousa treasure** from AD620, found near Keryneia, and some sets of Lusignan armour. From the roof there is a good view to the port and over the **old city**, the minarets acting as a reminder of its Ottoman past. Two mosques, the **Large Mosque** (Djami Kebir) and **Köprülü Hacı Ibrahim Ağa Camii** (Djami Jedid) lie to the east and west respectively, and many of the streets surrounding them still have Turkish names; there is a Turkish bath near Djami Kebir.

Folk Art Museum ★

An imposing old mansion at 253 Agios Andreou is the setting for this extensive collection of woodwork, jewellery, costume and domestic implements from the 19th and 20th centuries. It is open Monday–Friday 08:30–13:30 and 15:00–17:30 except Thursday afternoon.

To the northwest lies Platia Iroön, the centre of Lemesos's **red-light district**.

Archaeological Museum ★

At the far end of Agios Andreou, the Municipal Gardens, leading down to the seafront, are the setting for Lemesos's **Wine Festival** each September. The District Archaeological Museum is housed in a modern building here, and is open Monday–Friday 09:00–17:00, Saturday 09:00–17:00 and Sunday 10:00–13:00. It displays collections of finds from **Amathus**, **Kourion** (see pp. 74 and 78) and elsewhere. Room 1 concentrates on the Neolithic period, Room 2 on jewellery and pottery, notably from the Geometric era, and Room 3 on sculptures, of which those from Amathus reveal Egyptian as well as Greek influences.

(see pp. 74 and 78)

FESTIVALS

Lemesos has made a feature of a local love of festivals. In spring comes **Carnival,** with its grand parade and masquerade parties. In summer the **Lemesos Festival** attracts musical, dance and theatre groups from all over the world for performances in historic venues such as Kourion. In September there are the 10 nights of the **Wine Festival.**

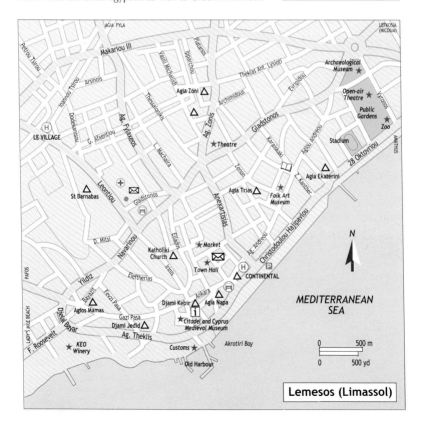

Lemesos (Limassol)

ST HELENA AND THE CATS

St Helena, mother of the Byzantine Emperor Constantine, apparently stopped in Cyprus in 324 on her return home from Jerusalem to Constantinople after a (successful) search to find the true cross, a fragment of which she deposited in Cyprus. She found the island gripped by the ravages of drought and, worse, overrun by venomous snakes. Her pragmatic solution was to return with a shipload of **cats** to hunt them down: the nuns at **Agios Nikolaos ton Gaton**, founded in the 4th century, still feed a horde of battle-scarred moggies, possibly the descendants of those original hunters, countless generations on.

AKROTIRI

The British RAF base dominates the Akrotiri peninsula, and its terrain is largely out of bounds to the casual visitor. In spring the ground beneath the trees within the security fences is a mass of **wild flowers**, in contrast to the goat-grazed pasture so often seen elsewhere on the island. The extensive **salt lake** lies outside the restricted area and is a favourite with visiting birders, especially during the spring and autumn when it becomes a resting-place for exhausted **migrant birds**. Through the winter and into early spring a distant raft of pink can be seen – but only a few lucky visitors see at close quarters some 10,000 **flamingos** which make the lake their temporary home. Between the lake and the security fence there is an area of grass and scrub which supports a rich flora, including **orchids** and turban butter-cups, and interesting fauna such as tiny green tree frogs and the occasional scorpion. If you stop here, make it clear to the guard at the entrance that it is to see the wildlife: it is as well to avoid any misunderstandings since security scares occur from time to time.

Much of the **Asomatos** marshland that once lay to the north of the salt lake has been taken over by the enormous **Fasouri** plantations which produce citrus fruit of all kinds. Roadside stalls in this area sell fruit at very low prices. Some small pockets of undisturbed wetland remain, though they take some finding: just south of the plantations a road leads west and then northwest towards the **Kouris River** and here birdwatchers may have the chance to observe egret, squacco heron and various migrant birds of prey.

The convent of **Agios Nikolaos ton Gaton** (St Nicholas of the Cats) is best approached from the southern end of **Lady's Mile Beach**. **Cape Gata** (Cape Cat) at the southern tip of the peninsula is at the end of a military runway and out of bounds: every autumn a colony of Eleonora's falcon raise their young here just in time for the winter migration.

Left: *Kolossi Castle, stronghold of the Knights Hospitaller.*
Opposite: *Feeding flamingos form a distant pink raft on the salt lake at Akrotiri.*

Kolossi Castle ★★

The square bulk of Kolossi Castle stands to the north of Fasouri, about 15km (9 miles) west of Lemesos. The castle had a long association with the **Knights Hospitaller**, granted land here by Hugo I in 1210, in return for their support against the Muslims. Building started in the late 13th century on the site of the camp of Isaac Comnenos.

Cyprus became the headquarters of the Order of the Knights of St John after the loss of Syria to the Arabs at Acre in 1291. The **Grand Commanderie** was established here until in 1310 the Knights founded their own state on Rhodes, but still administered their Cyprus lands from Kolossi. The original castle was damaged during raids by the Genoese and the Mamelukes; the three-storey fortified tower which still stands bears the coat-of-arms of the Grand Master Louis de Magnac, dating it at around 1454.

Many villages of the south were ruled by the Knights on a feudal basis and produced olive oil, wheat, cotton, wine and sugar. A **sugar factory** with a vaulted roof stands next to the main castle: the giant millstone lies outside close to the **aqueduct** which provided the water to power it.

The 12th-century church, **Agios Efstathios**, in the village outside the walls, was once the Knights' place of worship.

> ### COMMANDARIA
>
> The origins of this very highly rated, almost treacly brown dessert wine can be traced back to Crusader times. It is still produced from grapes grown in only a handful of villages (Kalo Chorio and Zoopigi amongst them) in the Troödos foothills. It may well have been Sultan Selim's fondness for Commandaria which precipitated the Ottoman invasion of Cyprus in 1570. Unaffectionately known as Selim the Sot, he died when drunk on Commandaria by slipping in his bath and fracturing his skull.

**LEMESOS TO PAFOS:
THE SOUTH COAST
Episkopi**

The area around the village of Episkopi has been a site of human habitation since Neolithic times. Traces of Stone Age settlements survive at **Erimi** and **Sotira** and at **Faneromeni** there is a Bronze Age settlement. Today the lively village has plenty of shops and several restaurants ably serving both the local Cypriot and the British Forces communities. The village also has a mosque and a small museum in an old house displaying finds from **Kourion**.

The **Sovereign Air Base** (SBA) is just like a little piece of Britain – as long as you ignore the different vegetation and perpetual sunshine. Even at the height of summer the green of well-watered playing fields in 'Happy Valley' contrasts sharply with the brown of the surrounding landscape. The area has its own police force, a mixture of British and Cypriot personnel who enforce speed limits rigorously.

Kourion (Curium) ★★★

The ruins of ancient **Curium**, which stand in memorable splendour high above the sea, are spread over three separate sites (open 08:00–19:30 in summer, until sunset in winter; entrance to the stadium is unrestricted). The visible remains date from the **Hellenistic** (Mycenaean and Dorian), **Roman** and **early Christian** periods. Traces of the earlier city kingdom of Kourion have eluded discovery.

If approaching from Lemesos, avoid the beach road and take the next left, Curium Theatre Road East. The **theatre** lies just beyond the car park within the precincts of the site. Built in the 2nd century AD, it was restored in 1960 and can hold 3500 people for plays and concerts. Mosaics thought to date from the 5th century are found in the **Annexe of Eustolios** which probably started life as a private dwelling before being converted into public baths. The mosaics show Christian influences in their use of fish, bird and floral motifs in contrast with the human figures of pagan designs.

The western part of the site, reached along a track from the car park, includes a **basilica** said to have been commissioned by Bishop Zeno in the 5th century. It is less impressive than the **atrium** next to it, which has mosaics and the remains of columns. Unfortunately for visitors, some parts of the site are often off-limits because of continuing excavation work.

Often overlooked but well worth visiting, the **stadium**, situated further north along the Pafos road, once sat 6000 people in seven tiers. Along its southern wall runs what remains of the aqueduct which carried water from the mountains to the city of Kourion. The **Christian basilica** to the east of the stadium seems to have been built to replace a pagan temple: in 1974 marble slabs on the floor were found to have come from the nymphaeum and to have been strategically placed to cover pagan scenes in earlier mosaics.

Tracing the path of the aqueduct to the west leads to the **Sanctuary of Apollo Hylates** dominating a small hill. The extant remains are from an early Roman building damaged in an earthquake in 365AD. However, worship on this site began as early as the 7th century BC: the deity Apollo Hylates was a fusion of the imported Greek god Apollo with a local woodland god.

KOURION'S ROLE

The **Ionic Rebellion** against the Persians in 498BC failed due to the treachery of **Stasanor**, King of Kourion, who changed sides during the battle of **Salamis**. Under the Roman Empire Kourion flourished and became a centre first for the worship of Apollo and then of Christianity. After the 7th century it declined when Arab raids forced the bishop and the population to move to **Episkopi**.

Opposite: *Raised walkways permit visitors to view the elaborate mosaic floors of the Annexe of Eustolios.*
Left: *The theatre in its imposing setting is Kourion's best known feature: concerts and plays are staged here throughout the summer.*

Above: *Governor's Beach is now reached by a fast new road from Lefkosia.*

South Coast Beaches

The attraction of **Curium Beach** is obvious when the sweep of sand towards the Akrotiri peninsula is seen from the archaeological site on the cliffs above: flags mark the part of the beach that is safe for swimmers. On the other side of the peninsula, **Lady's Mile** offers an extensive stretch of sand, but is hardly peaceful thanks to the noise of jets from the RAF base behind. **Dassoudi**, Lemesos's municipal beach, has a lot of sports facilities: beyond the Lemesos seafront many hotels boast 'beach facilities' – many have public access – and have appropriated strips of sand. **Governor's Beach** (Akti Kivernitou), some distance east of Lemesos and a favourite with locals and ex-pats, is reached along a track from the main road. The surface rocks are chalky white (there is a cement works at Vasiliko further along the coast) yet the sand, formed from underlying rocks, is dark grey.

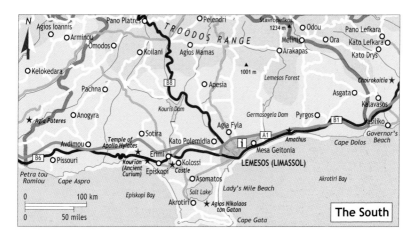

The South

Avdimou ★

The long sandy beach here shelves quite steeply offshore, and is reached by a 2km (1 mile) track from the main road along the coast. A well-shaded café provides a welcome respite from the alternate rigours of baking to achieve a sun-tan and swimming to cool down. **Avdimou village** lies north of the main road, and was an important settlement under Frankish and later Venetian rule. Philadelphus, one of the Ptolemies, is claimed to be its founder: he built it for his sister, Arsinoë.

Pissouri ★★

Until a decade or so ago Pissouri's claim to fame was the **Bunch of Grapes**, an inn in the true sense offering traditional food and accommodation. Now, the beach is dominated by a large luxury hotel complex and villas have sprouted on the hills either side of the valley down to the sea. The **beach** is good and **walks** along the scrub-covered clifftops are wonderful in spring, when the cistus is in bloom and a tiny, freesia-like gladiolus (*Gladiolus triphyllus*) flowers. From May when the **lammergeiers** (bearded vultures) arrive there is the added interest of watching the aerial displays of these winged giants which nest on the inaccessible cliff faces along this coast.

Petra tou Romiou ★★

Best seen on the journey to Pafos as the coast road hugs the white cliffs, for an hour or so before **sunset** the rocks are silhouetted by the scarlet globe of the sun dropping slowly to the horizon. Thanks to something as unromantic as atmospheric dust, sunsets here are spectacular, especially when, towards the end of summer, Saharan winds have whipped fine sand into the upper atmosphere and north-wards to Cyprus. A tourist pavilion with its own restaurant stands above the road from which there are good views over the coast below: the beach is reached via a subway.

Above: *Lofty white cliffs form the southern coastline between Lemesos and Pafos, an appropriate setting for the legendary birth of the goddess Aphrodite at Petra tou Romiou.*

THE APHRODITE CONNECTION

Petra tou Romiou is the legendary birthplace of Aphrodite. When the Titans hurled the severed genitalia of the unfortunate Uranus into the sea, she emerged from the resulting foam. The name, 'Rocks of Romios', derives from another legendary Cypriot, the Byzantine giant Digenis Akritas (Romios) who hurled rocks such as these at marauding Arab pirates and kept the Byzantine Empire intact.

Amathus ★★

The site of the ancient city kingdom of Amathus lies just north of the main coast road. Although excavations began only in 1980, many tombs had already been looted towards the end of the 19th century and, in an act of astonishing vandalism, much of the dressed stone from the site was used in the construction of the Suez Canal.

Although largely neglected after the 7th century, the city had been one of four administrative capitals in Roman times. It was also the birthplace of St John the Almoner, founder of the Order of the Knights of St John (the Knights Hospitaller) and the port remained in use until its destruction by Richard the Lionheart. The city was an important Phoenician trading base and retained its eastern links via the gods worshipped here, a mixture of Egyptian and Eastern as well as Greek. It also sided with Persia against the other cities at the Battle of Salamis.

Uncovered so far are the remains of a huge **agora**, a **Christian basilica**, an extensive **sluice system** and numerous **houses**, but the probable extent of what still lies hidden down to the coast is vast. During the construction of the Amathus Beach Hotel tombs were discovered and there are remains of **harbour walls** under the sea.

Choirokoitia ★★

Some of the earliest evidence of habitation on the island is found along the south coast. Two late Bronze Age cemeteries exist: at **Agious** and **Agios Dimitrios** (where two royal tombs have been found) near Kalavasos, where there was a copper mine. There are traces of even earlier, Stone Age, settlements at **Kalavasos-Tenta** and **Choirokoitia**. The foundations of the **rotundas** at Choirokoitia were discovered in 1936, but excavations began in earnest only in 1975. The settlement dates from the 6th or 7th centuries BC (open daily 07:30 to sunset).

The **Maroni River** in the valley below ensured a commanding defensive position, fertile land and a supply of smooth river stones for the foundations of the houses – mud bricks were added above.

Pano Lefkara ★★

To the east and away from the coast the land rises into the lower hills of the **Troödos** – this area is ideal for those based in Lemesos who want to explore small, country roads. In most of the valleys streams running down to the sea have been dammed (**fishing** is possible with a permit). The lake at **Germasogeia** is an attractive picnic spot.

From Kalavasos the road winds via Kellaki and the Orini region towards Melini and Odou; from **Choirokoitia** the same point can be reached via Vavla and Ora. Beyond **Odou** the vista compensates for a track which climbs dizzily in a series of sharp bends to the Troödos ridge and Pitsylia (*see p. 62*). The same route from Choirokoitia offers an alternative approach to Lefkara: via **Agios Minas** near Vavla (where nuns sell icons, an excellent honey and table grapes) to **Kato Drys**, birthplace of St Neofytos.

Of the two villages at Lefkara, the upper (**Pano Lefkara**) is more popular because of its lacemaking. The **House of Patsalos** (open 10:00–16:00 Monday–Saturday) contains a museum of the distinctive local lacemaking and silversmithing. Away from the centre, streets are narrow and houses have balconies and courtyards in Italianate style.

Kato Lefkara's alleyways are even more labyrinthine, with blue-painted houses. The church of the **Archangel Michael** has 12th-century frescoes.

THE LACEMAKERS

Lacemaking is a tradition said to have begun with the noblewomen of Lusignan and Venetian times. It is claimed that in 1481 Leonardo da Vinci bought an altarcloth made in Lefkara for Milan Cathedral. In summer the women work outdoors in groups producing their Lefkaritika and their menfolk sell it energetically both at home and abroad.

Opposite: *Remains of beehive-shaped houses dot the hillsides at Choirokoitia, one of the island's earliest known human settlements.*
Left: *A lacemaker demonstrates her delicate skill in Pano Lefkara, famous for centuries for this distinctive craft.*

Lemesos (Limassol) and the South at a Glance

GETTING THERE

Lemesos lies roughly equidistant between Larnaka International Airport, 70km (44 miles) away and Pafos Airport 63km (39 miles) to the west. All major tour operators operate transfer buses or arrange fly-drive. Independent travellers can hire vehicles via rental outlets at both airports or take taxis. Municipal buses run from both Pafos and Larnaka to Lemesos. Regular **ferries** operate to and from Greece (Piraeus, Rhodes, Iraklion, with various island stops *en route*), Israel (Haifa), Egypt (Port Said) and Lebanon (Junieh). CTO offices provide up-to-date listings and timetables on request. The port is about 4km (2.5 miles) from the town centre (on bus #1 during the day, #30 evenings).

GETTING AROUND

For drivers, the main island **motorway** routes connect Lemesos with Pafos, Larnaka, Lefkosia, and Ayia Napa. Transurban **bus** lines link Lemesos with Larnaka, Lefkosia, Pafos and the Troödos villages, with connections at Larnaka for Agia Napa and Protaras. Bus operators include **Intercity Buses**, tel: (24) 643492 between Lemesos and Larnaka; **EAL** tel: (25) 370592 between Lemesos and Lefkosia and for services from Lemesos to Platres and Troödos Square.

WHERE TO STAY

Lemesos boasts hundreds of hotels – most geared to the pre-booked package trade. For on-spec bookings try CTO at the airports: bargains are available out of season. Guesthouses in the bazaar cater for ferry passengers but you would be wise to avoid hotels in the red-light district.

LUXURY

Amathus Beach, Amathus, tel: (25) 832000, fax: (25) 832540, website: www.amathushotel.com 9km (6 miles) east of Lemesos. Well-established in extensive grounds; variety of water sports and activities for children and a recently upgraded Spa.
Four Seasons, tel: (25) 858000, fax: (25) 310887, website: www.fourseasons.com.cy Completely self-contained with a kindergarten for young children (2–10 years) and superb swimming pool.
Le Meridien, Amathus, tel: (25) 862000, fax: (25) 634222. 12km (8 miles) east of Lemesos. Virtually self-contained luxury resort with 3 restaurants, shopping arcade and a huge outdoor swimming pool.
The Londa, PO Box 52000, 4048, Limassol, tel: (25) 865555, fax: (25) 320040, website: www.londahotel.com This stylish new retreat on the sea in the city offers sweeping views out to sea, funky furni-ture, glittering lights and an outside area that leads immediately down to the pool and the Mediterranean.

MID-RANGE

Avenida Beach, tel: (25) 321122, fax: (25) 321123. A beach-front position in the Amathus district where most of the other hotels rate 5 stars.
Continental, Spyrou Araouzou 137, tel: (25) 362530, fax: (25) 373030. Interesting 1920s building, lively and well-patronized.
Le Village, 242 Leoforos Archiepiskopou, Leontia 1 Lemesos, tel: (25) 368126. Friendly, comfortable, unpretentious family-run, guesthouse.

BUDGET

Hellas Guest House, Zig Zag 9, tel: (25) 363841. In an old stone building, in the former Turkish district: cheap, clean and friendly.
Excelsior Guest House, Anexartisia 35, tel: (25) 353351. Friendly, cheap and cheerful.

Pissouri

Columbia Beach Resort, tel: (25) 833000, fax: (25) 833688, website: www.columbia-hotels.com Superbly situated in a bay with sandy beach and high white cliffs: good for water sports as well as a new Spa.
Bunch of Grapes Inn, PO Box 200, Pissouri, tel: (25) 221275. Restored farm-

house with rooms opening on to courtyard. Peaceful surroundings and very good food.
Kotsias, PO Box 120, Pissouri, tel: (25) 221014, fax: (25) 222449. Comfortable, well-appointed apartments with views over the bay.

CAMPING
Governor's Beach Camping, Pendakomo, tel: (25) 632300. 30km (19 miles) east of Lemesos. 360 lots.

Lemesos
Antonaros Tavern Attikis 5, tel: (25) 377808. Very popular, crowded and lively. There is no menu, just a superb *meze*.
Archipelago, tel: (25) 323670. In the old Amathus area – a real 'ethnic' village tavern serving good Cypriot food cheaply.
Asterias Fish Tavern, 55 Akademy Ave, Potamos tis Germasogeia, tel: (25) 326566. A very popular fish taverna in the main road serving a good variety of fish according to season.
Lefteris Tavern, Agias Christenis 4, Germasogeia Village, tel: (25) 325211. The restaurant is a warren of small, usually crowded rooms in a village house with good food and a predominantly ex-pat clientele.
Nitayia Far East Restaurant, 7 Saati, Old Port

Roundabout, tel: (25) 360671. A converted stone warehouse with vast aquarium tanks around the walls features a varied oriental menu (Thai, Japanese and Chinese). Very popular.
Ladas, Limassol old harbour, Potamos, tel: (25) 265760. Expertly refurbished restaurant that claims to be 'the oldest and most famous fresh fish taverna in Limassol'. The catch of the day is brought in from the port right next door daily and simply grilled or fried.
Xydas, Germasogeia Tourist Area, Pantheas, tel: (25) 728336. Modern fish restaurant with commanding views over the town: somewhat pricey by Cypriot standards but certainly well worth a visit.

Pissouri
Bunch of Grapes, Pissouri Village, tel: (25) 221275. A restored farmhouse. Very popular with the service community, the food is good but at a price.
Hani, tel: (25) 221211. On the Lemesos–Pafos road.

Very popular, it's basically a transport café serving very good Cypriot food.

Main tour operators offer a pick-up service from all Lemesos hotels with day and overnight excursions all over the island. Several operators offer 3-day tours to the **Holy Land** and the **Pyramids** – these are widely advertised in all hotels and travel agents.
Winery Tour: daily KEO tour of the Commandaria cellars in Franklin Roosevelt at 10:00. Booking is essential in the summer: tel: (25) 362053, otherwise meet in administration building reception area.

Tourist Offices:
15 Odos Spyrou Araouzou, tel: (25) 362756.
35 Odos Georgiou A, Potamos tis Germasogias, tel: (25) 323211 (opposite Dassoudi Beach).
Lemesos Harbour, tel: (25) 343868.
Lemesos General Hospital, tel: (25) 330777.

LEMESOS	J	F	M	A	M	J	J	A	S	O	N	D
AVERAGE TEMP. °C	17	17	19	22	26	30	32	33	31	27	23	19
AVERAGE TEMP. °F	62	62	65	72	79	86	89	91	87	81	73	66
SEA TEMP. °C	16	16	17	18	20	23	25	26	26	24	21	18
SEA TEMP. °F	61	61	62	64	68	73	77	79	79	75	70	64
RAINFALL mm	115	75	50	–	–	–	–	–	–	–	50	115
RAINFALL in	5	3	2	–	–	–	–	–	–	–	2	5

5
Larnaka
and the Southeast

Larnaka, number three in the island's hierarchy of towns, is barely half the size of Lemesos and has a local economy largely geared toward tourism. The main airport is sited on the coast just south of the town adjacent to the salt lake. The population has grown markedly, first as the result of an influx of Greek Cypriot refugees from Famagusta in 1974, followed by a steady flow of Lebanese Christians: today it stands at around 110,000.

Legend traces the origin of Larnaka to Kitim, son of Noah, who gave his name to **Kition**, the ancient site upon which present-day Larnaka grew up. Its history is chequered: after the colonization of the area by the Mycenaeans in the 13th century BC, Kition suffered the same fate as Enkomi and was destroyed by what Egyptian records term 'people from the sea'. By the 9th century BC the Phoenicians had made Kition an important trading centre, exporting copper from Tamassos. In 450BC the city, having sided with the Persians, suffered an attack from the Greeks.

Unlike Pafos, Kition did not enjoy prosperity in Roman times: it was destroyed by fire in 250BC. Over the 90 years during which the Genoese occupied Famagusta merchants fled to Kition and the town grew again. Under the Turks it became an important trading centre and became known by its present name, derived from 'larnax', a sarcophagus. During the 18th century foreign consuls were established here and a large foreign community gathered in Larnaka, but under British rule control passed to Nicosia.

DON'T MISS

*** **Beaches:** to the east of Agia Napa.
** **Hala Sultan Tekke:** the **flamingos** on the salt lake in winter.
** **Stavrovouni:** the view from the monastery.
** **Liopetri:** fishing boats arriving in the creek.
* **Agios Lazaros:** the church with its simple stone interior and belfry.

Opposite: *The serene 18th-century mosque of the Hala Sultan Tekke across the salt lake from Larnaka.*

THE CITY

The influence of Turkish rule is evident in the extensive area to the south of the town, which retains its Turkish street names. The **fort** (open Monday–Friday 09:00–19:00) was a former Lusignan castle rebuilt under Ottoman rule in 1625. It was later used by the British as a prison: the remains of a gallows can be seen by the entrance.

The nearby mosque of **Djami Kebir** was originally the medieval Church of the Holy Cross and was 'converted' by the Ottoman rulers. The local Muslim population which now uses it is Lebanese, Egyptian and Iranian. A second mosque, **Zuhuri Djami**, is now the youth hostel.

The hub of Larnaka's tourist industry, the palm-lined **Finikoudes** promenade runs along the seafront to the north of the fort, lined with cafés and English-style 'pubs'. The man-made beach is not among the finest in Cyprus but it is popular. The **harbour** is now equipped to function primarily as a yachting marina, with several hundred berths, although there are some ferries to the Lebanon.

The Pierides Museum **

Demetrios Pierides, a Cypriot scholar, founded this museum of antiquities in 1839 (open Monday–Saturday, 09:00–13:00; Sunday 11:00–13:00). Unlike other local museums, it shows artefacts from all over the island, many saved from tomb robbers by its wealthy founder. The collection is housed in an 18th-century townhouse and the exhibits range

from Neolithic pottery, through Archaic and Classical terracotta figures to Byzantine glass.

The **Larnaka District Museum** (open Monday–Friday 07:30–14:30, Thursday 15:00–18:00 except July and August) is better laid out than the Pierides Museum, but it cannot compete in terms of the wealth of the Pierides exhibits, but still merits a visit.

Left: *Agios Lazaros Church.*
Opposite: *The palm-lined Finikoudes promenade, popular for evening strolls.*

LAZARUS

It is said that Lazarus, raised from the dead at Bethany by Christ, was confirmed as a bishop in Cyprus by St Barnabas after his expulsion from Israel following his 'close encounter' with death. The church of **Agios Lazaros** was founded by Emperor Leo IV after a stone sarcophagus was found in 890 bearing the name Lazarus: the relics were plundered by Leo in 901 and taken first to Constantinople and then to Marseilles.

The Market ★

The main shopping thoroughfare Zinonos Kitios is close to the Pierides Museum and runs south to the **covered market** where, amongst the usual run of stalls you can also find copper and silver goods on sale, as well as **Laïki Geitonia**, a pedestrian precinct with restaurants, cafés and craft shops.

Agios Lazaros ★★

The church of Agios Lazaros was not 'converted' after the Ottoman conquest because in 1589 local Christians paid a heavy ransom to preserve it. But the interior is delightfully simple – the plain walls are the result of a fire in 1970.

Agia Faneromeni, to the west of Agios Lazaros, stands by a pair of rock-cut tombs. It is reputed to have curative powers – invoked by walking around the outside of the church three times and leaving behind an article of clothing.

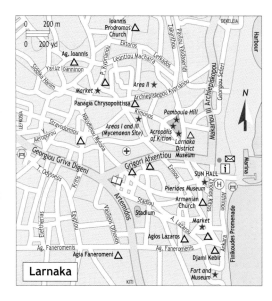

Larnaka

THE SALT LAKE

In winter and spring the extensive basins near Larnaka airport fill with salt water as it permeates the porous rocks which separate them from the sea. In summer the water evaporates and leaves a **salt crust**, which is still collected as it has been since Lusignan times, though now on a much smaller scale. In winter **flamingos** arrive and make the lake their home until March or April.

Kition ★★

Much of the ancient city kingdom of Kition lies beneath modern Larnaka. The remains date from distinctly different periods, which makes life confusing. Kimonos, running just west of the District Museum, passes **Pamboula Hill**: once an acropolis, its stones were removed in 1879 by the British, who were more concerned with eradicating malarial mosquitoes and used them to fill in some nearby marshes. The **Mycenaean** site (Areas I and III) near Panagia Chrysopolitissa was excavated in 1962 and yielded both pottery and jewellery. To the north, excavations are still proceeding in what is known as **Area II** (open daily, 07:30–14:30) on Leontiou Machaira. A catwalk takes visitors over part of a **Mycenaean** city built on top of an earlier settlement from 1300BC. Above this are the remains of the later **Phoenician** settlement, including a temple to Astarte.

CERAMICS

Kornos, just off junction 11 on the motorway, is a ceramics centre: ornamental troughs, garden pots, and huge storage vessels called *pithari*. Prices are very attractive but the difficulty of transporting goods home by air offputting. For those who settle in Cyprus this is the place to come to stock a patio. There is also a pottery at **Kofinou** to the south.

Hala Sultan Tekke ★★★

Across Larnaka's salt lake, set amongst palm trees, is the picturesque **Tekke**, or Hala Sultana Tekkesi, dedicated to **Umm Haram**, an aunt of the Prophet Mohammed who accompanied her husband in the Arab invasion of AD674, but fell from her mule and broke her neck. She was buried on this spot and, more recently, **Chadija**, grandmother of King Hussein of Jordan, was also buried here in 1930. In springtime the secondary grassland and the open pine plantations to the west of the Tekke are the home of many species of **wild orchid** which flower from January to April.

Panagia Angeloktistos ★★

In **Kiti**, 11km (7 miles) from Larnaka, the original 5th-century church of Panagia Angeloktistos ('built by angels') was destroyed by Arab invaders. Most of the present building dates from the 11th and 12th centuries, although some early **mosaics**, possibly from the 6th century, survive. They include one of the finest in Cyprus, depicting the two Archangels Michael and Gabriel.

Cape Kiti has beaches of indifferent quality – a mixture of sand and pebbles – though there are plenty of self-catering apartments and tavernas at **Perivolia**. There is a well-preserved **Venetian watchtower** north of the lighthouse and another at **Alaminos** west of Mazotos.

Above: *Angeloktistos church in Kiti, which contains some of the finest mosaics on the island.*
Opposite: *The Hala Sultan Tekke, an important shrine in the Muslim world.*

Stavrovouni Monastery ★★

The conical peak of **Stavrovouni** ('cross mountain'), isolated from the Troödos massif, rises 668m (2192ft) from the plain. At its summit is the oldest monastery in Cyprus, reached by the road from **Kornos** or, for the fit, by a steep path from **Agia Varvara**. Entry to women is prohibited, even though its foundation is attributed to a female, Empress Helena, mother of Constantine the Great, who left a splinter of the 'true cross' here when she was shipwrecked in AD327. It is claimed that this fragment, encased in silver and set in another cross, survived the destruction of the monastery by Arabs in 1426 and by Turks in 1570.

The monastery was rebuilt in the 1800s and today a small group of monks leads a rigorous life of work and prayer. Within is a grim collection of the skulls of monks, each with the individual's name carved on its forehead.

> **THE VIEW**
>
> On a clear day the panoramic view from the heights of Stavrovouni is remarkable. You will have to make the most of it while you are there as, unfortunately, photography is prohibited within the monastery and is also banned on the ascent because of the military camps situated nearby.

Pyrga ★★

Also reached via Kornos, Pyrga has a small Lusignan church dedicated to St Catherine. It is known as the **Chapelle Royale** after a wall painting of King Janus I and Queen Charlotte of Bourbon, under whose instruction the chapel was built in 1421.

BEACHES

Beaches around the southeast corner of the island are very good, with the **fine white sand** sought after by holiday-makers: in summer around Agia Napa they get very crowded and should be avoided by those seeking peace and quiet. A wide range of watersports, from pedalos to parascending, is available.

AGIA NAPA

Agia Napa is full of hotels, tourist shops, restaurants and cafés. With guaranteed sunshine, beaches and water sports of every description, there is plenty to offer families with children. There is no doubt that package tourism has brought prosperity but many middle-class Cypriots will talk about the mistake of allowing unbridled development in Agia Napa – the name means 'pleasant grove' – and cite it as an example of what to avoid. Others, scratching a living, would like a share of just that kind of action in their village, claiming the inalienable right to be allowed to make a fast buck too.

Since 1974 this area has seen more development than any other to cater for those who want sun, sea and hotel-based entertainment. In recent years Agia Napa has emerged as something of an oasis for fans of dance music with big name DJs and the international clubbing set flocking into the clubs.

Protaras ★★★

Just a few years ago Protaras was just **Fig Tree Bay** – a long stretch of sand, gently sloping to a crystal-clear sea named after the fig tree at the café claimed to have been brought from the east in the 17th century. The calm water and long run along the coast make it a favourite venue for **water-skiers**, while an offshore island affords some escape for swimmers from beaches which can get crowded in summer. The speed with which the town has grown is scarcely credible, and the strip of wall-to-wall hotels makes it difficult for non-residents to find the beach. Those who enjoy snorkelling or swimming off a rocky coast will find **Cape Gkreko** attractive when the sea is calm.

Left: *The monastery in Agia Napa is an unexpected haven in this resort.*
Opposite: *Sun and fun in Fig Tree Bay.*

Nissi ★★

Out of season it is possible to recognize what once made Nissi beach a quiet paradise. In season the fine white sands are scarcely visible between the closely packed bodies slowly frying in the sun, oblivious to any warnings about the thinning ozone layer. Agia Napa's three beaches – **Makronisos**, **Golden beach** and **Nissi beach** – are all linked by a paved walkway. Along the headland below the Grecian Bay hotel development are **sea caves** sculpted out of the white chalk cliffs.

Agia Napa Monastery ★★

In spite of development the centre of Agia Napa has retained some of its charm because of the monastery, dedicated to **Our Lady of the Forests**, which now serves as a conference centre for the World Council of Churches. Built during the 16th-century Venetian period, an arched cloister encloses a courtyard with a carved octagonal **fountain** whose waters are reputed to be therapeutic. Close by are the remains of a **Roman aqueduct**, built to carry the spring water. There is also a **folk museum**.

The main square outside the monastery becomes lively as evening approaches, with numerous bars, souvenir stalls and itinerant portrait painters.

ARCHAEOLOGICAL VANDALISM

Compared with the rest of the island there is a dearth of archaeological sites in this area. The blame falls on **Luigi Palma di Cesnola**, the American Consul based in Larnaka from 1865. He had the sanction of the Ottoman authorities to remove finds which he shipped off to the Metropolitan Museum of Art in New York. The destructive way in which he uncovered 12 temples and approximately 61,000 tombs made later excavation pointless.

THE KOKKINOCHORIA

Before 1974 and the subsequent vast expansion of tourist facilities in the area, the Kokkinochoria – literally 'red soil villages' – in the southeast of the island were regarded solely as the island's highly productive 'garden'. The rich soils, derived from weathered limestone with a high iron oxide content, are able to support up to three crops of potatoes in a single year. Unfortunately, excessive demands for water drawn from artesian wells lowered the water table and the supply became brackish. Now a system of reservoirs (the Southern Conveyor Project) ensures uncontaminated water for all-year-round irrigation. In the villages of the hinterland, life is based around agriculture, with **Avgorou**, **Liopetri** and **Xylofagou** being lynch-pins in the island's early potato production.

Pyla is unusual in that it is one of two mixed villages remaining in the south, although it has separate Greek and Turkish cafés. A silhouette of a Turkish soldier stands on raised ground as a characteristically 'macho' reminder. A much freer racial mixing is effected via the SBA at **Dekeleia**: here Turks and Greeks work together on the base and a taste of the southern nightlife is popular with Turks given a night out by their Greek colleagues. There is a lively black economy, with produce and 'designer label' clothing smuggled from north to south while electrical goods travel in the opposite direction – two communities working matters out on their own!

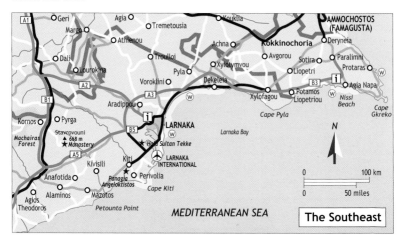

The Southeast

Several of the local churches are noteworthy: at **Sotira** there is the partly ruined **Agios Mamas** – the surviving frescoes date from the 16th century. The frescoes in the church of **Agios Georgios** at **Xylofagou** were damaged by fire and are still undergoing restoration. **Liopetri** has a 15th-century church, **Agios Andreas**, with an octagonal dome. Liopetri is also a centre for basket-weaving, as is **Livadia** to the north of Larnaka.

Liopetri Creek ★★

From Xylofagou early risers can make a detour to the narrow inlet at **Potamos Liopetriou**. Here in the dawn light you can watch small fishing boats bring their catch up the creek to their anchorage at the mouth of the Liopetri River, a world away from the nearby tourist resorts.

Deryneia

Famagusta is visible from this village, as is its ghost-town suburb of **Varosha** with its crumbling skyscraper hotels, looted and empty but for UN patrols since the invasion of 1974. The builders' cranes, visible through binoculars offered for hire in the cafés, stand as rusting sentinels.

Paralimni

Paralimni has always been a prosperous village, the more so in recent years as its dependency has changed from agriculture to tourism. On many maps a salt lake is marked to the west of the town. There are two large modern churches in Paralimni and a small 13th-century church which now stands in the centre of a traffic roundabout.

A GRIZZLY TRADE

Paralimni is infamous for its role in the lucrative 'ambelopoulia' trade. This gruesome practice involves the trapping of small, exhausted migrant birds (mainly blackcaps and other warblers). 'Lime sticks', covered with a sticky plant 'glue', are hidden in the scrub where the tiny birds stick fast; mist nets are even more efficient. The hapless victims' necks are wrung, and the pathetic corpses are pickled and eaten whole as a 'delicacy'. An estimated 4 million birds were caught each year, many of them exported to the Middle East. The Cyprus branch of Friends of the Earth launched a vigorous local and international campaign which has greatly reduced the annual carnage.

Left: *A flotilla of small fishing boats brings the daily catch up Liopetri Creek.*

Larnaka and the Southeast at a Glance

Larnaka International Airport is the island's main point of entry. Package operators provide hotel transfer or fly-drive on arrival. Municipal bus #19 runs into Larnaka 06:30–19:00 (Agia Lazarou Square) – bus terminals for connections to major towns are at the north end of the esplanade (Finikoudes). **Intercity Buses**, tel: (24) 643492, bus services between Larnaka and Lefkosia, Lemesos, Protaras and Agia Napa. **PEAL**, tel: (23) 821318, and **EMAN Buses**, tel: (23) 721321, operate to Protaras and Agia Napa. Long-haul shared **taxis** (4–8 passengers), operated by **PEYT** (Cyprus Interurban Taxis), leave every 30 minutes, 06:00–18:00, between Larnaka, Lemesos and Lefkosia; pick up and drop off anywhere within city limits. Larnaka: cnr Papakyriakou and Marsellou, tel: (24) 661010/(24) 777474; and at 2 Kimonos Str, tel: (24) 662110/(24) 777474.

Larnaca has a rather unreliable and slow city bus network but the historic centre is easily small enough to be walkable. Taxis are cheap and easy to hail or call **Acropolis Taxis**, tel: (24) 655555. **Hertz** has a 24hr car-rental counter at the airport, tel: (24) 643388. The bigger car rental agencies

have outlets at the airport, Larnaka, Agia Napa, Protaras and Paralimni: **Andy Spyrou Rentals Ltd**, Dekelia Rd, Shop 5, tel: (24) 645590, fax: (24) 644478; **Astra Self Drive** (Eurodollar International) Leoforos Artemidos 3, tel: (24) 624422/643203 (airport); **Hertz**, Leoforos Archiepiskopou Kyprianou 3, tel: (24) 655145, fax: (24) 656968/643388 (airport); **Thames**, Plateia Vasileos Pavlou 13, tel: (24) 656333, fax: (24) 657970/643044 (airport). There are smaller operators on Leoforos Archiepiskopou Makariou III.

Rural services operate to Paralimni (via Kokkinochoria) and to Pano Lefkara. A local service runs from Paralimni via Proteras to Agia Napa.

In season there is little chance of on-spec accommodation in luxury or mid-range hotels, and **pension** accommodation is also limited. Many **self-catering apartments** are pre-booked in high summer but are glad of bookings at other times.

Larnaka
LUXURY
Golden Bay Beach Hotel, Dekelia Rd, tel: (24) 645444, fax: (24) 645451. Good beach. Well-appointed, all amenities. **Louis Princess Beach**, Voroklini, Larnaca, tel: (24) 645500, website: www.louishotels.com Top-quality; outskirts of town;

two poolside wings; long, empty beach; choice of restaurants, bars, water sports and activities for children. **Lordos Beach Hotel**, Dekelia Rd, tel: (24) 647444, fax: (24) 645847. Large, friendly; reasonable beach, water sports.

MID-RANGE
Larco, Umm Haram St, tel: (24) 657006, fax: (24) 659168. In old Turkish quarter; good value. **Sun Hall Hotel**, Athens Ave, tel: (24) 654431, fax: (24) 652717. On the seafront – handy for the marina.

BUDGET
Youth Hostel, Nikolaou Rossou 27 (nr Agios Lazaros, tel: c/o (22) 442027. Open all year, 07:30–23:00. **Sandbeach Castle Hotel**, Piyale Pasha, tel: (24) 624706. Comfortable; good value; a little noisy; on waterfront, sea-facing rooms have great views. **Livadhiotis Hotel Apartments**, Roussou 50, tel: (24) 626222. Self-catering and one-bedroom apartments; affordable, historic centre of town.

Agia Napa
LUXURY
Grecian Park Hotel, Cape Greco, Protaras, tel; (23) 832-000. Between Agia Napa and Protaras; refurbished landmark hotel; wonderful views; sandy beach; huge pool. **Olympic Lagoon Resort**, Agia Napa, tel: (23) 722500. Huge resort; ideal luxury choice for

families; multiple activities; pools, tennis, snooker, crèche.

MID-RANGE
Anesis Hotel & Apartments, PO Box 59, tel: (23) 721104, fax: (23) 722204. Very close to Grecian Bay and the beach.

Protaras
LUXURY
Capo Bay, PO Box 115, tel: (23) 831101, fax: (23) 831110. Gardens overlook Fig Tree Bay.
Crystal Springs, PO Box 246, tel: (23) 826900, fax: (23) 826901. Friendly hotel above a small cove and far enough out of town to escape crowds.
Vrissiana Beach, PO Box 29, tel: (23) 831216, fax: (23) 831211. Entertainment for children; good water sports.

MID-RANGE
Chrysland Cove, PO Box 239, tel: (23) 831600, fax: (23) 831 605. Away from centre; good facilities; man-made beach.
Domniki Beach Apartments, tel: (23) 832800. Right on the coast – 50m from Fig Tree Bay.

WHERE TO EAT

Larnaka
Restaurants along the **Finikou-des** are all much the same – sit wherever you find a table.
Flamingoes Restaurant Café, Hala Sultan Tekke; good Cypriot fare. Next to salt lake, great for naturalists: flamingos on lake, orchids in woods nearby.
Pyla Tavern, Dekelia Rd, tel: (24) 653990. Popular with

Cypriot families, offers fish in season beautifully cooked.
Miliges, Bia Pasha 42, tel: (24) 655867. Modern building; traditional food, particularly meat.
Monte Carlo, Piale Pasha 28, tel: (24) 653815/629504. Good Cypriot food – especially the meat *meze*; seafront restaurant; balcony extends over sea.
Tudor Inn, 28A Lala Mustafa St, tel: (24) 625608. Incongruous 'Swiss Chalet' appearance, quite expensive. Food well cooked and presented.

Agia Napa
Le Bistro, Odysseus Elytes 11, tel: (23) 721838. Charming old house; international menu; superbly cooked food.

Protaras
Anemos Beach Restaurant, tel: (23) 831488. Next to Capo Bay Hotel above Fig Tree Bay. Good food, efficient service and great views over the bay.
The Dragon 2, tel: (23) 831414. Good Chinese food.
Sandinavia Mini Golf, tel: (23) 513115/823886. Near Profitis Ilias on main road. Fast service and generous helpings of pizzas and pasta.

Vindobona, tel: (23) 831448. Main road to Agia Napa. Viennese food accompanied by (taped) Viennese music.

Paralimni
Platsa Tavern, Arch Kyprianos 1, tel: (23) 821350. Good traditional village cooking; overlooks busy square.
O Costas Sas, tel: (23) 821474. Deryneia–Sotira highway. No proper menu but selection of traditional *meze* dishes; meat features prominently.
Vangelis, Griva Digeni Ave 40, tel: (23) 821456. Noisy and often crowded; family restaurant patronized by locals; good, reasonably priced Cypriot food.

TOURS AND EXCURSIONS

Main tour operators offer pick-up service from all hotels with day and overnight excursions.
Larnaka General Hospital, tel: (24) 800500.

USEFUL CONTACTS

Tourist Offices: Platia Vasileos Pavlou, **Larnaka**, tel: (24) 654322. Larnaka International **Airport**, tel: (24) 643000 (24 hrs). Leoforos Archiepiskopou Makariou 17, **Agia Napa**, tel: (23) 721796.

LARNAKA/ AGIA NAPA	J	F	M	A	M	J	J	A	S	O	N	D
AVERAGE TEMP. °C	17	17	19	22	26	30	32	33	31	27	23	19
AVERAGE TEMP. °F	62	62	65	72	79	86	89	91	87	81	73	66
SEA TEMP. °C	16	16	17	18	20	23	25	26	26	24	21	18
SEA TEMP. °F	61	61	62	64	68	73	77	79	79	75	70	64
RAINFALL mm	115	75	50	-	-	-	-	-	-	-	50	115
RAINFALL in	5	3	2	-	-	-	-	-	-	-	2	5

6
Lefkosia (Nicosia)

This bustling, cosmopolitan city with a population of 200,000 is firmly divided, with Greeks and Turks separated by a 'buffer' zone: the **Green Line** passes through the heart of the old city and is maintained by the United Nations. The city is set on the **Mesaoria**, the fertile plain between the Troödos and the northern ranges which early writers described as being a mass of scarlet poppies and wild tulips in spring. Nowadays, with intensive weed-free cultivation, it is a wall-to-wall blanket of green.

In 1995 it was decided that Nicosia, the name given to the city by its European conquerors, should be replaced. The southern part of the divided city is now known locally by its Greek name Lefkosia (Turkish Lefkoşa). Its origins can be traced back to the 4th century BC when it is thought that Lefkos, son of Ptolemy, rebuilt and expanded the ancient settlement of Ledra which lay on a Neolithic site.

Lefkosia's true prosperity dates from the 7th century, when coastal settlements fell victim to Arab raids. During the Lusignan period the royal court was established in the city and many of its impressive public buildings were constructed, in spite of frequent earthquakes and several outbreaks of plague. In 1426 the Mamelukes conquered the city, forcing on it a period of Egyptian rule. Lefkosia held out under siege for six weeks in 1571 when some 20,000 people were slaughtered by the Ottoman Turks. It endured a very uneasy peace under the Ottoman Empire, with riots in 1764 and the execution of Archbishop Kyprianos in 1821.

DON'T MISS

*** Cyprus Museum: island's finest archaeological collection.
** Famagusta Gate: the magnificent eastern entrance.
** House of Hadjigeorgakis Kornesios: an opulent Ottoman mansion.
** Laïki Geitonia: stroll around the attractive shops.
** Makarios III Cultural Centre: the gallery displays an impressive icon collection.

Opposite: *Bayraktar Camii marks the place where the flag-bearer of the Ottoman invaders scaled Lefkosia's walls in 1570.*

THE CITY

The magnificent **Venetian Walls** encircling the old city replaced the original Lusignan fortifications after the Venetians assumed power in 1489, and were greatly strengthened in the 1560s. Around the circumference of 4.5km (2.8 miles) stand 11 heart-shaped bastions. There were originally three gates into the city: **Pafos Gate** (Porta Domenica) to the west; **Keryneia Gate** (Porta del Proveditore) to the north; and the **Famagusta Gate** (Porta Giuliana) to the east. The wide moat below the walls is now utilized for coach and car parks and as gardens below the **Costanza Bastion**, where the **Bayraktar Mosque** marks the suicide mission of the first Ottoman to scale the walls, and the **Podocataro Bastion**.

Above: The D'Avila bastion. Of the 11 bastions, five each lie in the north and south with one in no-man's land.
Right: The Famagusta Gate is a popular cultural centre.

The City Centre

Lefkosia within the walls is sufficiently compact to explore on foot (the CTO and the Bank of Cyprus provide free maps showing places of interest both within and without the walls). A good starting-point is Platia Elefterias, main point of entry into the old city: start and finish your walk in **Laïki Geitonia**. Once part of Lefkosia's red-light district, this area has been reincarnated as a pedestrian precinct with craft shops and pavement restaurants: perhaps a bit twee for the architectural purists but a pleasant place in which to wander or sit and watch the world go by. Following the success of this venture large parts of the old city are being tastefully restored.

The Green Line lies at the end of **Odas Lidras** (once known as 'murder mile' for the number of British troops ambushed along its length). Before you reach the line, turn east along Nikokleous to **Faneromeni Church** (built in 1872) with the tiny **Arablar Mosque** behind it. In the maze of streets close to the Green Line almost every old doorway conceals an artisan of some sort. Here too is the municipal **Market**, with fruit and vegetables brought in by the most amazing collection of village buses. Eventually, heading roughly east, you'll see the Archbishop's Palace ahead; the **House of Hadjigeorgakis Kornesios** is towards the south past the coffin-makers (see p. 98).

Patriarch Grigorios runs westwards from here to the **Omeriyeh Mosque** (once a 14th-century Augustinian church but mostly destroyed by Ottoman artillery and rebuilt by Mustafa Paşa in 1571) and the **Turkish Bath**. By continuing in the same general direction you come to **Trypiotis Church**, built in Franco-Byzantine style by Archbishop Germans II in 1695. Turn left into Onasagoras to arrive back in Laïki Geitonia where you can take a break for a well-earned cool beer.

For the more energetic the walk can be extended via a diversion northeast from the Archbishop's Palace first to the city's finest church, **Panagia Chrysaliniotissa** ('Our Lady of the Golden Flax'), begun in 1450, and then along the walls to the **Famagusta Gate**.

(see p. 98)

A TIME OF HARMONY

Archbishop of Austria, Ludwig Slavator, visited the city in 1873 and described 'Venetian fortifications beside Gothic edifices surmounted by the Crescent, on antique classic soil. Turks, Greeks and Armenians dwell intermingled, at heart bitter enemies, united solely by their love for the land of their birth.'

Above: *Shopping in Onasagoras Street: few real bargains but plenty to grab the attention.*

THE CULTURAL CENTRE

The **Famagusta Gate** on the Caraffa Bastion has been restored to become the Lefkosia Municipal Cultural Centre. Beyond the impressive gateway (bearing six coats of arms) is a vaulted passage now used as a venue for exhibitions, lectures, conferences and concerts. The curved ceilings make for good acoustics.

THE GRAND DRAGOMAN OF CYPRUS

The Dragoman was the official intermediary between Orthodox Christians and their Ottoman rulers, but was effectively a tax collector appointed by the Sublime Porte. **Hadjigeorgakis Kornesios** was Grand Dragoman of Cyprus from 1779 to 1809. Famed for his linguistic skills, he grew exceptionally rich from his estates, helped by his tax-exempt status. Following a peasant revolt in 1804, he fled to Istanbul where, eventually running out of friends and favours, he was beheaded in 1809 after dabbling in intrigues against Sultans Selim III and Mustafa IV.

The Leventis Museum ★★

Within easy reach of Laïki Geitonia, this museum (open 10:00–16:30 Tuesday–Sunday) brings the best in modern display techniques and technology to nearly 4000 years of life in Lefkosia. The exhibits include ancient artefacts, noblemen's costumes from the Lusignan period and early books which refer to the island.

The Archbishop's Palace and Cathedral ★★

Several of the city's museums lie inside the walls in **Kyprianos Square**. The complex of buildings includes both the new palace, built in neo-Byzantine style in 1961, and the old building it replaced. Within the palace, the **Makarios III Cultural Centre** (open 09:00–13:00 and 14:00–17:00 weekdays, Saturday 09:00–13:00) houses an art gallery (with maps and lithographs as well as paintings), libraries and the **Byzantine Museum**, which holds the island's largest collection of icons.

The small cathedral of **Agios Ioannis**, which was built at the instigation of Archbishop Nikiforos in 1662, stands between the old and new Archbishop's palaces. Inside, its series of 18th-century frescoes depicting biblical scenes have recently been restored.

Below: *The Archbishop's Palace, part of a large complex in the old city.*

The Folk Art Museum ★

The old palace, once part of a 15th-century Benedictine monastery, is now the home of the **Folk Art Museum**

(open 08:30–13:00 and 14:00–16:00 weekdays, Saturday 08:30–13:00): the collections include woodcarving, pottery, tapestry and embroidery, and national costumes. The **National Struggle Museum** next door has assorted memorabilia depicting the struggle for independence from 1955–59.

SHOPPING

Although much of greater Lefkosia is modern and a brash testament to the use of concrete in terms of its architecture, shopaholics will find plenty of diversion along Makarios III Avenue and the adjoining streets.

Within the walls good buys, including leather bags, jackets and shoes, can be found along the bustling thoroughfares of Odos Lidras and Onasagoras. Designer spectacles cost half as much as elsewhere in Europe – bring your prescription or take a new test – and will be ready in 24 hours.

The House of Hadjigeorgakis Kornesios ★★

Lying roughly to the south of the Archbishop's palace (and easier to reach on foot because of a tortuous one-way system) is this exquisite Venetian mansion. Built in the 15th century but with later Ottoman additions, it has been restored to house the award-winning **Cyprus Ethnographic Museum** (open Monday–Friday 08:00–14:00, Saturday 09:00–13:00). The collection documents the lives of the privileged during the Ottoman period.

The Cyprus Museum ★★★

Outside the walls near the Pafos Gate, the large cool building of the Cyprus Museum houses, within its 14 rooms, the finest discoveries from sites all over the island (open 09:00–17:00 Monday–Saturday, 10:00–13:00 Sunday and public holidays). Here is arguably the best **archaeological collection** in the Middle East, spanning over 7000 years of history from Neolithic times (6800BC) to the early Byzantine period.

Amongst the thousands of items on display, don't miss the collection of red and white pottery and soapstone figures from the Neolithic site at Erimi, or the group of around 2000 votive figurines from Agia Irini dating from the 7th and 6th centuries BC. Mycenaean bowls inlaid with gold and the green **'Horned God'** came from ancient Enkomi, while the marble statue of **Aphrodite** from Soli, dating from the 1st century AD, is frequently used as a symbol of the island.

The **Municipal Theatre**, with its columned, neo-classical façade, sits almost opposite the Cyprus Museum in the well-kept **Municipal Gardens**. Next to it is the **House of Representatives**. **St Paul's Anglican Cathedral**, built to serve the personnel of the British Administration, is just to the south of the Museum.

IDALION

Idalion was a centre of the Aphrodite cult where **Adonis**, the lover of the goddess, was supposedly killed while out hunting wild boar. Tradition has it that the red anemones in spring mark the spots where his blood fell. According to legend, the son of Idalion and Adonis, Golgos, founded the settlement of Golgoi near Athienou, to the north-east of Dali. The infamous *Palma di Cesnola* (see p.90) dug out large sculpted heads and complete statues here which he shipped off to New York.

LEFKOSIA DISTRICT

Many of the archaeological sites on the Mesaoria lie to the north of Lefkosia, cut off by the division. To the southwest, you have first to escape the urban sprawl of the suburb of **Strovolos** to reach **Fikardou**, **Tamassos**, **Agios Irakleidios** or **Machairas** (*see pp.* 64–5). En route, near the village of **Deftera**, is an enlarged natural cave which is a place of early Christian worship dedicated to **Panagia Chrysospiliotissa** (Our Lady of the Golden Cave), but the interior paintings are now damaged.

The main road to Troödos passes the impressive buildings of **Kykkos Metochi**, an annexe of Kykkos Monastery (*see p.* 61) built in the 19th century to administer its extensive landholdings. The Kykkos Monastery Research Centre lies about 6km (4 miles) further along the Troödos road in the Byzantine **Archangelos Michail Monastery**, founded by Archbishop Nikiforos (whose tomb is in the narthex) and rebuilt in 1650 and 1713.

Villages to the South

From the Lemesos–Lefkosia highway take the Nisou turning to reach **Pera Chorio**, where the church of **Agii Apostoli** contains frescoes dating from the 12th century. **Dali**, the village to the east, has a small 14th-century (1317) sandstone church. Outside the

village is the Bronze-Age site of ancient Idalion, one of the city-kingdoms: it is not yet fully excavated but some parts of the ancient walls can be seen.

Alampra, to the south of Nisou, is another Bronze-Age site still under excavation: in general, the area between Lefkosia and Lemesos, around Kalavasos and Choirokoitia (*see p.* 78), has revealed some of the oldest traces of human habitation in Cyprus.

Left: *Dividing north from south, the Green line has only one crossing for day visitors near the old Ledra Palace hotel in Lefkosia.*
Opposite: *A single olive tree near Dali village.*

GOING NORTH

Visitors to the south are permitted, under current regulations, to make **two day-trips** on foot into the north during their stay (possibly more if you have a genuine historic or other interest and you are persuasive). Since the north is regarded both by the south and internationally as an **illegal port of entry**, visitors to the north are *not allowed to travel south*. Limited permission is given to some residents (Turks resident in the south, Maronites) to travel north, but no Greek Cypriot can travel north and if you have a **Greek or Armenian name** forget it whatever your nationality.

Border regulations are subject to change so always check before planning a trip. The **only crossing** is at the Green Line on the western side of the old city walls of Lefkosia near the Ledra Palace Hotel. At the **first checkpoint** the Greek authorities take a note of your passport number and accommodation in Cyprus. Cross the UN-held 'no-man's land' to reach the **second checkpoint**, the Turkish one, where you obtain a day visa – passports are not stamped. The crossing opens at 08:00 and closes at 17:30: **check carefully** as times can change and on occasions the border is closed. No overnight stays are permitted and goods bought over the border are not officially allowed into the south. Money, including CY£, can be changed (quietly) everywhere.

CYPRUS HANDICRAFTS

For gifts with a Cypriot flavour take a taxi to the **Cyprus Handicrafts Centre** on Athalassa Avenue (turn right at the lights at the beginning of the Lefkosia–Lemesos highway). In workshops set around a quiet courtyard, are weavers, potters and woodcarvers, all of them displaced from the north. The centre has retail outlets in **Laïki Geitonia** and in all the major towns.

Lefkosia (Nicosia) at a Glance

GETTING THERE

With Lefkosia International Airport closed since 1974, **Larnaka Airport**, 49km (31 miles) away, is the main point of arrival. Most people making Lefkosia their destination will book fly-drive, hire via rental outlets at the airport or take a taxi into the city. To reach Lefkosia by **bus**, take the municipal bus #19 (which runs from 06:30 to 19:00) from Larnaka (Agios Lazaros Square): bus terminals for connections to major towns are at the north end of the esplanade (Finikoudes).

GETTING AROUND

Interurban bus services are operated by **Intercity Buses**, tel: (22) 665814, between Lefkosia and Larnaka. **EAL buses** run between Lefkosia and Lemesos. **NEA AMOROZA** runs between Lefkosia and Pafos via Lemesos. **PEYT** (Cyprus Interurban Taxis) operates to all towns from Lefkosia (Leoforos Salaminos-Municipal Parking Place, Kolokasi, tel: (22) 730888/(22) 777474). Urban buses serve outlying districts of Lefkosia from Plateia Solomou, west of Plateia Eleftherias, tel: (22) 473414, but within the walls of the old city walking is the only practical way of getting around.

WHERE TO STAY

Unless your visit coincides with a international fair or some such gathering it is usually possible to find accommodation in Lefkosia on spec or through the **CTO** office at Larnaka Airport. Several mid-range hotels and guesthouses exist in the old city – if you can put up with the problems of mosquitoes and restaurant noise after midnight.

LUXURY

Cyprus Hilton, Leoforos Archiepiskopou Makariou, PO Box 2023, tel: (22) 377777, fax: (22) 448858. Popular with visiting dignitaries: the city's premier hotel with facilities (and prices) to match.
Hilton Park Nicosia, Grive Dighenis Ave, tel: (22) 695111, fax: (22) 351918. International chain hotel outside the centre, popular with businessmen.
Holiday Inn Nicosia City Centre, Rigainis 70, tel: (22) 712712. Far and away the best hotel in the old town, with an (indoor) swimming pool and gym, rooftop brasserie, and modern rooms, the Holiday Inn is built virtually in the walls of the old city.

MID-RANGE

Cleopatra, 8 Florina St, tel: (22) 445244, fax: (22) 452618. Close to the main business and commercial areas.

Classic Hotel, Rigianis 94, tel: (22) 664006. A comfortable, slightly oddball hotel with pretensions above its price band, just within the gates of old Nicosia, the Classic is stylish without being over-costly and has an excellent restaurant.

BUDGET

Regina Palace, Riyenis 42–44 and Fokionos, tel: (22) 463051. Within the red-light district but friendly and well-placed for exploring the old city.
Sans Rival, Solonos 7C, tel: (22) 474383. A rather comfortable guesthouse within Laïki Geitonia, and handy for a vast choice of local restaurants.
Venetian Walls, Ouzounian 38, tel: (22) 450805, fax: (22) 473337. Situated as the name suggests within the old walls – a good base from which to explore the old city.
Youth Hostel, Odos I. Hadjidaki 5, off Odos Themistokli Dhervi, tel: (22) 444808/442027. Open all year, 07:30–23:00.

WHERE TO EAT

Abu Faysal, Klimentos 31, tel: (22) 760353. Atmosphere is informal and lively; situated in a fine old house with an art gallery: authentic Lebanese cuisine served to a cosmopolitan clientele.
Astakos, Menelaos 6, tel: (22) 353700. A fish

restaurant serving an excellent *meze* among other dishes: popular with locals and expatriates alike.

Armenaki, Sans Souci 15, tel: (22) 378383. Unpretentious, serving authentic Armenian dishes: popular with the locals.

Brown's New Café Restaurant, 13 Stassinou. Classy new brasserie, bar and nightspot with cosmopolitan atmosphere and occasional live jazz.

Chang's China Restaurant, Acropolis 1, Engomi, PO Box 4976, tel: (22) 351350. Friendly and efficient Chinese restaurant – large tables with rotating centres make it popular for family outings.

Erenia, Leoforos Archiepiskopou Kyprianou 64A, Strovolos, tel: (22) 422860/496080. Only 15 tables in an old taverna serving what the 'cognoscenti' regard as perhaps the best *meze* in Lefkosia – the *bourekia* are legendary.

Fytron Chytri 11, tel: (22) 461466. Vegetarian wholefood at lunchtime with suppers on selected nights.

Cyprus Hilton, Leoforos Archiepiskopou Makariou, tel: (22) 464040. The Cyprus Hilton holds 'International speciality' evenings with generous buffets, for example, 'Fish' or 'Cypriot'.

The Konatzin, Delphi 10, tel: (22) 446990. Very

popular, especially for its *meze*. Serves both traditional and vegetarian fare.

Mama's Kitchen, Acropolis 44A, tel: (22) 353093. Traditional home-cooking from a take-away with a menu that changes daily. Open at lunchtimes – including Sunday – it is deservedly popular so expect to queue.

Mattheos, Pl 28 Oktovriou, tel: (22) 475846. Behind Faneromeni Church, it opens at 04:00 to cater for municipal market traders: there is always something special in the cooking pots – a real taste of old Lefkosia and the long-gone *mayirka* (kitchens).

Navarino Wine Lodge, Navarino 1, tel: (22) 780775. A good buffet; tables set out in a lovely garden.

Plaka Taverna, Engomi, tel: (22) 477840. A definite contender in the best *meze* stakes: friendly, good service, excellent food.

Psarolimano, Odos 28 Oktovriou 59, tel: (22) 350990. Speciality fish restaurant. Dishes change according to the season – the red mullet is superb.

Skaraveos, Nikokreontas 4, tel: (22) 765190. Very popular with the locals – make your selection of fish from the chilled cabinet to be beautifully cooked.

Skorpios, Stassinos 3, Engomi, tel: (22) 351850. Operates in conjunction with Skorpios bar and discotheque: upmarket French and Cypriot fare. Often very busy.

TOURS AND EXCURSIONS

Main tour operators offer a pick-up service from all Lefkosia hotels with day and overnight excursions all over the island.

Organized **walking tours** of the city start from the CTO in Laïki Geitonia: check with them for details of routes and times.

For more information on day-trips to the **north**, *see p. 101.*

USEFUL CONTACTS

Lefkosia General Hospital, tel: (22) 801400.

Tourist Offices, Leoforos Lemesous, 19, tel: (22) 451994, fax: (22) 485337. Laïki Geitonia, tel: (22) 444264. Postal enquiries: PO Box 4535, Lefkosia.

LEFKOSIA	J	F	M	A	M	J	J	A	S	O	N	D
AVERAGE TEMP. °C	15	15	18	23	28	32	35	35	32	27	22	17
AVERAGE TEMP. °F	59	60	64	73	82	90	95	95	89	81	71	62
HOURS OF SUN DAILY	5	6	7	8	10	12	12	12	10	9	6	6
RAINFALL mm	60	35	35	-	-	-	-	-	-	-	25	75
RAINFALL in	2	1	1	-	-	-	-	-	-	-	1	3

7
The North

The persistent memory of the north is the dramatic crags of the **Keryneia** range. The limestone peaks run from Livera in the west to the tip of Karpas, the island's easternmost point. The mountains are always visible: from the plane of the Mesaoria to the south or as a backdrop to the resorts of the northern coast. The north is largely untouched by the development which has overtaken the south: towns and villages have retained their charm and the hospitality of Turkish Cypriots can be overwhelming.

It is impossible to ignore Turkish military presence in the north when attempts to wander off the beaten track can bring you to a military post, apparently in the middle of nowhere. Some Turkish Cypriots maintain that Turkish military presence is necessary to bring peace of mind. Understandably, memories of EOKA activities die hard and more than two decades of non-contact between Greeks and Turks in Cyprus have meant that the Turkish Cypriots have no means of recognizing that *énosis* now has negligible support in the south where the economy is vibrant.

The main reason for the military presence is the north's heavy economic reliance on Turkey. The military occupancy and the large numbers of Anatolian settlers brought into northern Cyprus together create a constant tension. Turkish Cypriots have good reason to claim that they are treated unfavourably compared with mainland Turks. Everything possible has been done to eradicate all traces of both Greek and British influence – especially in place-names – and to emphasize the Turkish nature of the north.

TURKEY

Ammochostos
(Famagusta)

CYPRUS

MEDITERRANEAN SEA

DON'T MISS

*** **Selimiye Mosque** (Agia Sofia), Lefkoşa.
*** **Belapais Abbey:** beautiful 13th-century abbey.
*** **Lala Mustafa Paşa Mosque:** (Cathedral of St Nicholas), Famagusta.
*** **Salamis:** famous archaeological site.
** The **Crusader Castles** of the northern range.
** The **Keryneia Shipwreck** in Keryneia Castle.
** **Vouni:** ancient ruins in a truly dramatic setting.
* The **Caravanserais** in Lefkoşa.

Opposite: *The timeless harbour and castle in Keryneia.*

LEFKOŞA: THE NORTHERN PART OF THE CITY

First impressions after crossing no-man's land are of the number of young Turkish soldiers and a generally down-at-heel appearance typical of any mainland Turkish town. The distinct advantage of the lack of development is that **old buildings** remain untouched, through inertia rather than by design (cynically referred to in the south as Attila the Conservationist). Lefkoşa has a population of around 60,000 – one third of the population of the north (and only a quarter that of the southern part of the city).

It is easily possible to see Lefkoşa in a morning on foot thanks to the concentration of **Gothic** and **Ottoman** monuments most of the sights can be found just by wandering through the maze of narrow streets lined with tiny shops which contribute to the charm of the old city.

The Arabahmet Mosque ★

This imposing mosque stands not far from the Turkish checkpoint. It was built in the 17th century in memory of a conqueror of Cyprus, **Ahmet Paşa Arab**, and restored in 1845. It is a dramatic building with a high minaret, a large single dome and three smaller domes over the entrance porch. The tomb of Kâmil Paşa, Grand Vizier of the Ottoman Empire and the only Cypriot ever to hold this office, stands in the courtyard, along with several other tombs and a fountain. Preserved within the mosque is a single hair reputed to be from the head of the Prophet Mohammed.

The Selimiye Mosque ★★★

Several mosques are clustered together near the centre of the old city, the finest being the Selimiye Mosque, known as the **Cathedral of Agia Sofia** until 1954, even though the Ottomans added the two

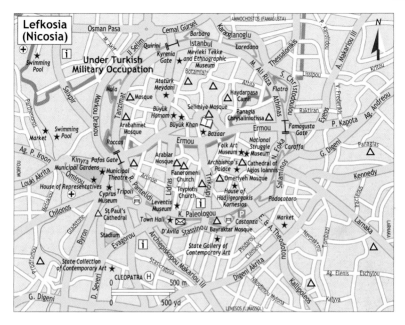

minarets which dominate the city and made it their main mosque in 1570. The conversion also involved painting the inside white and removing any statues or other images idolizing the human form – tombstones were taken out or used to pave the floors. (Shoes should be removed before entering the mosque and silence observed if your visit coincides with one of the five daily prayer times.)

The construction of the cathedral began in 1209 and even when it was consecrated in 1326 the building had still not been finished. In this cathedral the Lusignan princes were crowned **Kings of Cyprus**: a second coronation in Famagusta followed to endow the honorary title King of Jerusalem.

The design is clearly French despite the Ottoman additions: high vaulted arches are set on massive pillars and the west façade is dominated by a triple sculpted portal with an immense circular window set above it. Gold and precious stones set into the aisle were plundered by the Genoese during their invasion in 1373.

Opposite: *The Cathedral of Agia Sofia became an Ottoman mosque in 1570.*

DERVIŞ PAŞA KONAĞI

Derviş Paşa was the publisher of the first Turkish newspaper in Cyprus. His former home in Beliğ Paşa Sokağı has been well restored and is now an **ethnographical museum** (09:00–19:00 in summer; 09:00–13:00 and 14:00–16:45 in winter) housing a collection of basketry, copperware and embroidery in addition to early copies of his newspaper. The house was built in 1807.

Selimiye Square ★★

The **Sultan Mahamut Library** is an octagonal domed building standing just east of the mosque, with an impressive collection of religious manuscripts. The old Venetian house across the roundabout is the **Lapidary Museum** which contains carvings from tombs and churches and incorporates a beautiful Lusignan Gothic window rescued from demolition. (Both collections are open Monday–Friday, 07:30–14:00 and 15:30–18:00.)

From here it is a short walk to the **Haydarpaşa Camii**. Formerly the Lusignan church of St Catherine before its adoption by the Ottoman Turks, it is now an art gallery.

To the south, between the Selimiye Mosque and the market, the **Bedesten** began life as a 6th-century Byzantine church, was rebuilt in the 14th century as the Church of St Nicholas of the English and was briefly used as the Orthodox cathedral during Venetian rule. There are six Venetian coats of arms above the north door. It became a covered bazaar after Ottoman occupation (*bedesten* means a cloth market).

The **Belediye Pazari**, the large covered market, is a hive of activity in the early morning, with stalls selling crafts and other goods as well as fruit and vegetables.

Below: *A member of the Mevlevi order, popularly known as the 'whirling dervishes'.*

Ataturk Square ★

Between Selimiye and Ataturk Square, along Asmali Street, lie a number of **Ottoman** buildings. The **Büyük Hamam** began life in the 14th century as the Church of St George of the Latins. From Ottoman times until today it has served as a public bath and is the largest in the north of the city.

Ataturk Square was the centre of Turkish life in the city long before partitioning occurred. It is a bustling place, with its British-built administrative buildings in classical style. The so-

called **Venetian Column** in the middle of the square is a granite column originally from Salamis, erected here by the Venetians. From the square, the main road out of town is the former Keryneia Avenue.

The **Keryneia Gate** (Porta del Proveditore), northernmost of the three gates into the city, now stands isolated since the British cut into the walls on either side of it in 1931 to widen access for traffic. The original gate is surmounted by a square chamber added in 1821 when it was repaired by the Turks.

Turkish Ethnographic Museum ★
Just before you reach the Keryneia Gate is the 17th-century **Mevlevi Tekke**. Now a museum (open Monday–Friday, 07:30–14:00 and 15:30–18:00) it has collections of glass, metalwork, costume and musical instruments, but until 1954 it was the monastery of the Mevlevi sect, the '**whirling dervishes**'. Devotees spun in their giddy dances on the lower floor to the music played in the gallery above.

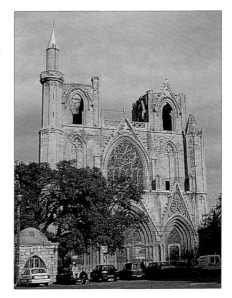

Above: *Famagusta's magnificent Lusignan cathedral of St Nicholas.*

FAMAGUSTA

Overlooking the bay to which it gives its name, Famagusta, now known in the north as **Gazimağusa,** owes its foundation to Ptolemy II in 285BC. It has suffered a chequered history since that time, with several periods of prosperity punctuated by raids and destruction. **Ammochostos** (the old Greek name meaning 'city sunken in the sand') received an influx of Greek refugees when Salamis fell to Arab raiders. An Armenian influx occurred in 1136 by order of the Byzantine emperor. Following the fall of Acre in Syria in 1291 the population grew once again and so did Famagusta's importance as a centre of trade because of

> **WHIRLING DERVISHES**
>
> The **Mevlevi sect** followed the teachings of Celaleddin Rumi, the Mevlâna who came from Balkh in Central Asia to live in Konya in Anatolia during the 13th century. He taught that humankind was separated from God while living on earth, but could be reunited with him through music and dance – ideas alien to the Muslim orthodoxy of the time. The sect survived in Cyprus until 1954, long after having been banned in Turkey by Ataturk.

Right: *Famagusta's Citadel is known as Othello's Tower. The city claims to be the setting for Shakespeare's play.*

its natural deep water harbour. Many of its buildings were constructed during the Lusignan period. Genoese and later Venetian traders grew fabulously wealthy in Famagusta, as apparently did the majority of its courtesans.

The old city can be explored by walking around the walls with their 15 bastions, starting with the Lusignan **Citadel**, otherwise known as **Othello's Tower** (from its Shakespearian connections). According to legend, a fortune still lies within in the citadel, hidden there by Venetian merchants who were forced to flee empty-handed from the Ottomans.

Lala Mustafa Paşa Mosque ★★★

This magnificent edifice, originally the Gothic Lusignan **Cathedral of St Nicholas**, was built between 1294 and 1326. Kings of Cyprus received the crown of Jerusalem here as an honorary title. The frontage has three porticoes and an enormous window with a central rose; one of the twin towers, partially demolished during the Turkish siege, was converted into a minaret. All the columns within the building are painted white and tombstones set into the floor are covered with prayer mats. The sycamore fig tree outside is reputed to have been planted when the cathedral was built.

A succession of Venetian governors took occupation of the **Palazzo del Proveditore** across the square: its last occupant was the poet Namik Kemal, imprisoned there by the Sultan in 1873 for writing a play regarded as seditious. The **Town Hall** served the Ottomans as the Sinan Paşa Mosque and was used by the British administration as a store for potatoes – it was built in the 14th century as the **Church of St Peter and St Paul**.

Salamis ★★★

In its heyday, **Salamis** was one of the most important of the ancient city kingdoms. Under Roman rule it remained the main commercial centre, in spite of Pafos being the official capital, largely because of its harbour. In Byzantine times Salamis was renamed Constantia and once again became the capital of Cyprus.

Left: *The Roman paleastra, or exercise ground, is bordered by this wonderful Byzantine colonnade.*

It is arguably the island's finest archaeological site, much of it still uncovered. It occupies about 5km² (2 sq miles) and also has superb beaches to the east.

The much photographed Roman **Paleastra** or exercise ground, with its rows of stone columns and marble floor, stands behind the tourist pavilion and marks the site of the **Gymnasium**. To the south are the thermal **Baths**, with fragments of mosaic still decorating the walls. Parts of the hypocaust which heated the various halls can be

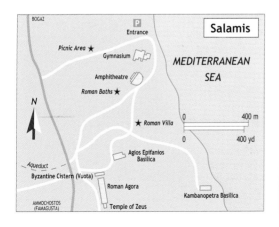

seen under the floors. From here a paved way leads past colonnades to a magnificent Roman **Amphitheatre**, built in the reign of Augustus, with seating for 15,000. To the east of the site are the remains of an **aqueduct** which brought water from Kythrea to the cistern (*vuota*) near the **Agora**.

There are two basilicas standing amongst the ancient remains on the site. The one to the west near the Agora is dedicated to **Agios Epifanios**, where mosaic floors cover a crypt stripped of its contents. The other is the 4th-century **Kambanopetra basilica** overlooking the sea, where stone jetties, traces of the ancient port, are visible in the lagoon.

Apostolos Varnavas Monastery ★

Near the locked southern gate of the Salamis site, opposite the Cistern, a road leads west to this former monastery. The buildings date from 1756, and were erected on the foundations of a 5th-century church built to house the bones of St Barnabas. An archaeological museum containing local finds (open daily, 08:00–18:00) is now housed in the cells.

ST BARNABAS

Barnabas, companion to St Paul in his missionary work, was stoned to death in about AD75 at the hands of the Salamis Jews, who objected to his activities. Legend has it that St Mark, cousin of Barnabas, hid his bones in a nearby rock-cut cave. About 400 years later, Barnabas appeared in a dream to **Anthemios,** Bishop of Salamis, revealing his burial place. The subsequent discovery of these relics impressed Emperor Zeno sufficiently for him to grant self-determination to the church.

The Royal Tombs ★★

The Royal Tombs opposite the monastery are **Mycenaean**, and date from the 7th and 8th centuries BC. Of some 150 tombs many had already been looted before the site was excavated in 1957. They are regarded as important for the light they throw on Mycenaean funerary rites. The remains include the skeletons of horses sacrificed (together with chariots and several servants) after their owner's cremation for use in the hereafter.

Egkomi-Alasia ★★

The remains of the Bronze Age city of **Alasia** lie southwest of Salamis off the road to Lefkoşa. Achaean Greeks from the northern Peloponnese are thought to have founded it around 2000BC, bringing with them the Mycenaean culture. The first written references to Alasia, on Egyptian documents, refer to it as a thriving port exporting copper to Egypt (at a time before the sea receded when the river Pedeios was navigable). When the site was first excavated it was thought to be a vast **necropolis** serving Salamis, but it was later realized that the inhabitants buried their dead beneath their floors as at Choirokoitia (*see p. 78*). A statue of the horned fertility god which used to be worshipped here is now in the Cyprus Museum in Lefkosia.

THE KARPAS PENINSULA

The Karpas peninsula, the 'panhandle' to the northeast of Cyprus, is not open to day visitors from the south. A continuation of the limestone ridge of the northern range, its springtime wild flowers are superb, provided settlers' flocks have not got to them first. It is a first port of call for migrant birds arriving on the island: **rollers**, **golden orioles** and **bee-eaters** are the most colourful of visitors. **Turtles** are known to breed here, particularly along the long sandy beach stretching to the monastery of **Apostolos Andreas**. Before 1974 Karpas was dotted with a mixture of Greek and Turkish villages, most of which have since been peopled by settlers from mainland Turkey. Three Karpas villages (**Rizokarpaso**, **Agios Andronikos** and **Agia Trias**) still have residual, though diminishing, Greek populations. The ancient, isolated churches of the peninsula are either locked, like **Panagia Kanakaria**, or have been desecrated: the 10th-century **Agios Fotios tis Selinias** is now a cowshed.

THE CASE OF THE KANAKARIA MOSAICS

There are numerous early Christian sites on the Karpas peninsula. One of them, **Panagia Kanakaria**, hit the news when mosaic panels stolen out of the church after 1974 fell by a tortuous route into the hands of an American art dealer who offered them for sale to the Getty Museum. The legitimate government of Cyprus sued in the American courts for their return and won the case in 1989. Numerous other thefts of antiquities have taken place, some with the proven connivance of discredited UN officials.

Opposite: *The partially restored Roman amphitheatre at Salamis once had the capacity to hold crowds of up to 15,000.* **Left:** *The limestone crags of the dramatic northern range, home of vultures and other birds of prey and the soaring backdrop to all the sights of the north.*

Right: *The walls and towers of St Hilarion castle seem to grow out of the crags – legend tells of a secret door to an enchanted garden.*

CRUSADER CASTLES

Three famous castles enjoy incomparable vantage points spread along the northern limestone range.

Kantara **

Easternmost of the three, Kantara lies at 610m (2000ft) and is most easily approached from Famagusta. Its name is from an Arabic word for a bridge. It dates from 900 and is traditionally where Isaac Comnenos fled in 1191 when pursued by a furious Richard the Lionheart. The Lusignans rebuilt and expanded it but it was then largely dismantled by the Venetians, who considered its 'technology' obsolete. However, they left most of the outer fortifications which include an impressive barbican and square tower. The views from it are spectacular, with both coasts of the Karpas peninsula visible as they converge.

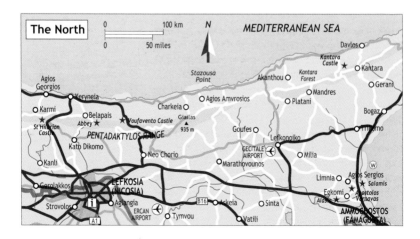

The North

MEDITERRANEAN SEA

Voufavento ★★

The two other castles are best approached from Keryneia: they were built within sight of one another and used beacon fires as an early warning system against pirate raids. Voufavento, in its lofty position at 940m (3100ft), is appropriately named 'wind-buffeted'. The Lusignan gatehouse is reached after a steep walk. Few of the original hundred or more rooms remain, but the balcony offers marvellous views to the west and St Hilarion. The remains of a church stand at the top of a crag, where there is also a viewing platform.

The direct route from the south is blocked by the Turkish military, who have commandeered **Chrysostomos Monastery**, once famous for its holy spring. The road via **Klepini** affords the best approach.

Above: *The Crusader castles were sited to give warning of invaders – now they provide breathtaking views.*

St Hilarion ★★

The road from Keryneia climbs towards the needle peaks of **Pentadaktylos** – this and their Turkish name, Beşparmak, both mean 'five fingers'. At the watershed the road to the west leads to St Hilarion, also known at different times as Didymus and Dieudamour. Castle walls and towers seem to grow out of the rocks, producing a building out of fairy tales on a crag 732m (2400ft) above the plain. The massive walls, much restored, are Byzantine, but much of the rest, on three distinct levels, dates from the 13th century. A double gateway leads to a barbican and gatehouse. On the upper level are the royal apartments, with breathtaking views from the elegant Queen's Window.

St Hilarion, after whom the castle was named, was a 7th-century hermit who lived and died in these mountains. First a monastery and then a fort grew up around the site of his tomb. Throughout its early history the castle was seen as an impenetrable retreat and doubled as a summer palace for the Lusignan kings. The Venetians dismantled it in part, but in 1964 it was briefly used again as a stronghold by a group of the TMT, the Turkish Cypriot equivalent of EOKA.

A mountain road, built during the colonial administration, runs westward from St Hilarion via the highest point, Kyparissovouno, at 1023m (3356ft), for some 29km (18 miles) along the top of the range, giving incomparable views right and left.

> ### NORTH CYPRUS HERBARIUM
>
> Halevga (now signposted Alevkaya) is a worthwhile detour. For those equipped with lunch there is a large picnic site; for naturalists there is the North Cyprus Herbarium set up in the old Forestry Station by Dr Deryck Viney. The surrounding countryside is superb for plants, especially orchids such as the endemic Cyprus bee orchid (*Ophrys kotschyi*).

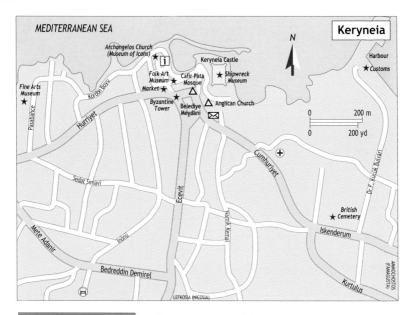

Keryneia

MEDITERRANEAN SEA

SETTLERS

After 1974 mainland Turkey unashamedly used the north of Cyprus as a social dumping ground for military veterans, Anatolian peasants, urban poor, psychiatric cases and some criminals. The long-suffering Turkish Cypriots, alarmed by this practice, formed an active opposition which succeeded in stopping it. No official figures are admitted, but the number of settlers is estimated at between 30,000 and 80,000, plus vast flocks of goats which have caused considerable eco-logical damage.

Opposite: *Keryneia, the jewel of northern Cyprus.*

KERYNEIA AND THE WEST

Keryneia is now called **Girne** within North Cyprus. It owes its foundation to Arcadian Greeks and was an important colony around 1200–1000BC, although little remains from those or later Roman times, when it was called **Corineum**. Walls and towers constructed by the Byzantines to fend off pirate raids became the base for Venetian development. Under the Ottoman rulers Keryneia declined, but when the British arrived it became a favoured haunt of returning colonials, many of whom stopped off on the way home and never left: the idyllic **harbour** has changed little since colonial times.

Keryneia Castle ★★

Guy de Lusignan attacked the castle in 1191 and sub-sequently used it as a prison. Later it found favour as a safe royal residence, especially when the peasants showed any sign of revolting. From 1464 the castle fell into Venetian control and it was strengthened: parts of the structure dating from Byzantine, Lusignan and

Venetian times are all visible to the tutored eye. The Ottoman Turks used it to house the tomb of one of their generals, Sadik Paşa; the British subsequently used it as a prison for EOKA fighters until 1950. Today it is a museum (open daily 08:00–13:00 and 14:00–17:00) best known for the unique ship it contains within its walls.

The Keryneia Ship ★★

In the late 1960s a merchant vessel dating from the time of Alexander the Great was found in water 33m (108ft) deep, complete with a cargo of Rhodes wine in 404 amphorae, almonds in jars and 29 millstones. The hull was raised during 1968–69 by a team under the supervision of Vassos Karageorgis, Director of the Antiquities Service. Evidence from coins and radiocarbon dating showed that it sank some time in the 3rd century BC when it was already approximately 80 years old, creaking its way from Anatolia via Samos and Rhodes to Cyprus. It had a single sail 10m by 6m (33ft by 20ft), was 14.75m (48ft) long and 3.5m (11ft) wide. It is the oldest shipwreck ever discovered.

The Harbour ★★

Nowadays Keryneia's harbour deals only with pleasure craft, boat trips and visiting yachts. The best view is from the former Byzantine church of Archangel Michael, now a **Museum of Icons** (open daily, 09:00–13:00 and 15:00–17:00).

The **Folk Art Museum** (open daily, 09:00–17:00) close to the harbour used to be a grain store; it houses a collection of various handicrafts, mainly from the 18th century. The nearby **Cafir Paşa Mosque** dates from the Ottoman period.

BEACHES

The better beaches lie to the east of Keryneia. **Acapulco Bay** has a hotel complex and a sandy beach which shelves gently, making it safe for children. **Turtle Bay** is a nesting-site for loggerhead turtles but there is as yet no conservation project here to protect the hatchlings. For the connoisseur, the best beaches are on the **Karpas** – tiny sandy coves where you will be the only ones on the beach. The beach near the site of **Salamis** is worth visiting, and between Salamis and Boğaz there are also sandy coves. On the south side of the peninsula there are some lovely beaches beyond the dunes that line parts of the shore west of **Cape Apostolos Andreas**.

BITTER LEMONS

The villages, lifestyle and land-scapes around Belapais in the mid-1950s have been immortalized by **Lawrence Durrell** in the classic *Bitter Lemons*, published in 1957. He lived in the village of Kazaphani (now signposted Dogamköyist) until the EOKA violence and the retaliation shattered his idyll and he left. Many British expatriates stayed on after 1974: some, including a few British MPs, have moved in since, joining the 'ancient Brits'.

Below: *Once seen, never forgotten, the ruins of Belapais Abbey have a majesty few places in Cyprus can match.*

Belapais Abbey (Beylerbey) ★★★

With its majestic arches and windows, located between the Pentadaktylos to the south and the sweeping coast to the north, the abbey of Belapais is one of the island's most atmospheric sites.

Augustinian monks fleeing from Palestine founded it in the early 13th century. It was taken over by the Premonstratensians (a reformed branch of the order) whose white habits led it to be known as the White Abbey. Its present name derives from the Lusignan title **Abbaie de la Pais**. The site was later despoiled and used as a convenient source of stone into the early days of the British administration.

Through the arched gateway is the 13th-century church, well-preserved and usually kept locked. The 14th-century cloisters lie beyond the church, with bosses carved with human and animal heads. The marble sarcophagus from the 2nd century AD was once used as the communal wash-basin. The crowning glory is the refectory window, from which the snow-capped peaks of Turkey's southern Taurus range, just over 64km (40 miles) away, can seem very near on a clear day.

The abbey is best visited on a weekday to avoid the crowds; if possible aim to be there in the early morning or evening when the ruins take on a golden glow.

Soli ★★

Legend has it that Soli, one of the ten city-kingdoms of ancient Cyprus, was founded in the 6th century BC and named after **Solon**, the Athenian statesman and poet who had been summoned to the island by King Philokypros. In fact, there was probably a settlement here much earlier. Soli was the last city to hold out against the Persians in 498BC. It grew prosperous, especially in Roman times, on the copper mined at **Skouriotissa**.

Left: *The mosaics in the Christian basilica at Soli include striking and beautiful animal motifs.*

It is scarcely credible that large quantities of stone were removed from the site by the British to line the Suez Canal, but in spite of this depredation Soli is worth visiting. On a high slope are the remains of an amphitheatre while lower down varying religious influences have left behind a 5th-century Christian basilica, with striking mosaics, and temples dedicated to Isis and Aphrodite from 250BC. The famous statue of **Aphrodite**, symbol of the island and now in the Cyprus Museum in Lefkosia, was found here.

Vouni ★★

Although only the foundation walls are now visible at Vouni, the palace built in the 5th century BC, its commanding position 250m (820ft) above the sea makes the site very impressive. The quantities of sculpture, coins and jewellery found during the excavations, many of them Persian, indicate the wealth of the settlement.

MORFOU

This quiet town with its bewildering maze of streets was once the centre of one of the richest areas in Cyprus. Local farmers became millionaires from the quantity and quality of citrus fruit they produced. Now the orchards look run-down: the Turkish Cypriots who came here from the south were primarily from wine-growing regions. And an uncertain future has not helped, since proposals for settlement have usually cited Morfou's return to Greek hands as a condition.

Left: *The evocative setting of the ruined palace at Vouni.*

The North at a Glance

GETTING THERE

The north is accessible to visitors from the south for day visits (*see p. 101*). **Those arriving directly in the north are not allowed into the south. When planning a trip north, check current regulations.**

Ercan, a small, modern airport lies 24km (15 miles) east of Lefkoşa, 51km (32 miles) from Famagusta, 37km (23 miles) from Keryneia. Direct flights on Turkish Airlines (THY) link travellers with airports in Turkey (Adana, Ankara, Antalya, Istanbul and Izmir). No bus service from the airport: courtesy buses are provided by main tour operators, or go by taxi (agree on a price first).

Ferries, run by Turkish Maritime Lines, ply between Keryneia and Tasucu on Turkish coast (daily, 4½ hours). There is a daily service between Famagusta and Mersin in Turkey and daily express services in summer between Keryneia and Alanya, Antalya and Alanpur.

GETTING AROUND

The north is served by an extensive **bus network** operating on a 'flexible' timetable throughout the day (stop early evening – check return times) and are very cheap. There are frequent services between towns: **Lefkoşa–Keryneia** and **Lefkoşa–Morfou** (Güzelyurt) from terminal near Keryneia Gate. **Lefkoşa–Famagusta**: terminal on Mehmet Münir Mustafa. **Bus stops** (*otobus*

durak) are marked; rural buses stop on demand.

Taxis display a yellow 'TAKSI' sign on the roof and congregate at ranks in towns. There is an official tariff. **Dolmuşes** (shared taxis) follow set routes, are cheap, and set off when full (*dolmuş* means 'stuffed').

Car-rental agencies include: **Keryneia: Riverside Rent a Car**, tel: (0392) 821 8906/7; **Cyprus Car Hire**, tel: (0392) 815 2508. **Lefkoşa: Sun**, Apdi Ipekçi Caddesi, tel: (020) 78787. **Famagusta: Atlantic**, Sinan Paşa Sok, tel: (036) 63277; **Deniz**, Yeniboğaziçi (near Salamis), tel: (036) 65510; **Sur**, Ismet Inönü Bulvari, tel: (036) 65600.

WHERE TO STAY

Most visitors stay near **Famagusta** or **Keryneia**. **Lefkoşa** has modest hotels and tends to be a day-trip destination. Following 1974, Greek-owned hotels were seized: those listed are new (post-1974) or have always been Turkish-Cypriot. **Pansiyons** (pensions): cheap, clean but basic; details from Northern Cyprus tourist offices.

Lefkoşa
Saray, Ataturk Meydanı, tel: (0392) 228 3115, fax: (0392) 228 4808. Casino and very good rooftop restaurant.

Keryneia
Chateau Lambusa, tel: (0392) 821 8751. One of the best hotels in Northern Cyprus;

comfort and quality; beach.
The Colony, tel: (0392) 815 1518. North Cyprus's newest, most luxurious hotel; superb pool terrace; Keryneia centre.

Famagusta
Bilfer Palm Beach Hotel, tel: (0392) 366 2000, fax: (0392) 366 2003. Full range of facilities including gym, medical service and courtesy bus to town.
Altun Tabya, Kızıl Küle 9, Kaleiçi, tel: (0392) 366 5363. A typical 'commercial' hotel in the old part of the town.

SELF-CATERING
Cyprus Gardens, tel: (037) 12552/12722, fax: (020) 83739. Secluded, well-designed; water sports; sandy beach.
Long Beach, tel: (037) 88282. Bungalows with restaurant, sandy beach and windsurfing.

CAMPING
Two purpose-built seaside camp sites, both with restaurants (smaller sites around coast):
Riviera Bungalows, tel: (0392) 822 2026. 5km (3 miles) west of Keryneia; rocky coast. Tent spaces and small chalets.
Onur Camping, tel: (0392) 227 6898. North of Salamis Bay Hotel; under pines; sandy beach.

WHERE TO EAT

Lefkoşa
Annibal, Saraçoğlu Meydanı (off Istanbul Caddesi). Traditional kebab house in old city.

The North at a Glance

Kibris Ashevi, 39A Ataturk Avenue, tel: (0392) 223 1751. Oven-cooked dishes; very popular (must book in advance); surpisingly affordable.
Saray Hotel, Ataturk Meydanı, tel: (0392) 228 3115. Rooftop terrace with views over old city.

Famagusta
Cyprus House, opp. County Court Building, tel: (0392) 376 6459. Athentic Turkish-Cypriot restaurant; old village home. Highly recommended.
Erich's Pub, Salamis Road, tel: (0392) 366 6214. Pub food and good cold lager beer; congenial atmosphere; a long-established Famagusta watering hole.
Eyva, Salamis Rd, tel: (0392) 378 8235. Friendly; unpretentious; Turkish-Cypriot food.
Onur, tel: (0392) 822 2026. Attached to Onur camp site. Lively and friendly; traditional food, music and dancing.

Keryneia
Altinkaya 1, tel: (0392) 821 8341. 8km (5 miles) west of Keryneia; a deservedly popular fish restaurant.
Antis Taverna, Keryneia Harbour, tel: (0392) 822 2256. A firm favourite; local food, lively atmosphere and live music.
Carob Club, Keryneia Harbour, tel: (0392) 815 6277. A rooftop bar with live music and harbour views, a fine Turkish-Cypriot restaurant, the Ocakbasi, an indoor bar and café.
Chinese House, Karaoglanou Ave, tel: (0392) 815 2130.

Cantonese and Peking dishes.
Courtyard Inn, tel: (081) 53343. In Karakum, 2.5km (1.5 miles) east of Keryneia. Tables in courtyard garden. Mainly French food. (B&B available.)
Efendi's House, Old Turkish Quarter, tel: (0392) 815 1149. In an old house; pretty courtyard for outdoor dining.
Halils, Kondon Boyn Caddesi, tel: (081) 52299. Traditional Turkish food on the quayside.
Harbour Club, tel: (081) 52211. Next to castle; local dishes downstairs on pavement, French menu upstairs; items on menu on the expensive side.
Niazi's Restaurant & Bistro, City Centre, tel: (0392) 815 2160. Opp. Dome Hotel; central steakhouse; fine grill menu.
Paradise Restaurant, tel: (081) 52356. In Çatalköy (east of Keryneia). Friendly; often crowded; good cheap *meze*.

Belapais
Abbey House, Belapais, tel: (081) 53460. Close to Abbey in old house and garden – always full. French cuisine, expensive by local standards but worth it.
Altinkaya 2, Bellapais Rd junction, tel: (0392) 815 5001.

Close to Bellapais village; poolside bar; fine seafood restaurant.

For day trips to ancient sites (**Belapais**, **Salamis**, **Soli** and **Vouni**) and the **Keryneia range** (castles), try: **Unwin Holidays**, Keryneia, tel: (0392) 822 3508; **Ya Ya Tours**, Lefkoşa, tel: (0392) 228 5357; **North Cyprus Rentals**, Keryneia, tel: (01420) 473 193; **Apple Tour**, Keryneia, tel: (0908) 155 499; **Can Tourism**, Lefkoşa, tel: (0392) 228 73333, Keryneia, tel: (0392) 815 2245.

Ministry of Tourism, website: www.holidayinnorthcyprus.com
Lefkoşa Hospital, 51 Girne Caddesi, tel: (0392) 228 5441.
Akçiçek Hospital, Cumhuriyet Caddesi, Keryneia, tel: (0392) 815 2266.
Famagusta Hospital, Polat Pasa Bulv, tel: (0392) 366 5328.
Tourist Offices: Ercan Airport, tel: (023) 14737; **Famagusta**, Fevzi Çakmak Caddesi 5, tel: (036) 62864; **Keryneia**, Kordon Boyu 30, tel: (081) 52145; **Lefkoşa**, in Ministry of Tourism, tel: (020) 75052/3.

KERYNEIA	J	F	M	A	M	J	J	A	S	O	N	D
AVERAGE TEMP. °C	17	17	19	22	26	30	32	33	31	27	23	19
AVERAGE TEMP. °F	62	62	65	72	79	86	89	91	87	81	73	66
SEA TEMP. °C	16	17	17	19	21	24	26	28	26	25	22	18
SEA TEMP. °F	61	62	62	65	70	75	79	82	79	77	72	64
HOURS OF SUN DAILY	6	7	8	10	12	13	13	12	11	9	8	6
RAINFALL mm	115	75	50	–	–	–	–	–	–	–	50	115
RAINFALL in	5	3	2	–	–	–	–	–	–	–	2	5

Travel Tips

Tourist Information
The Cyprus Tourist Organization (CTO) produces free accommodation directories, maps and brochures. CTO has offices in every large town in the south of the island, at both airports and in Brussels, Paris, Frankfurt, Amsterdam, Tokyo, London and New York.
The North: maps, booklets and lists of accommodation are available from Tourist Offices at Ercan Airport and large towns (see p. 121), and in London and New York. For further details contact the Ministry of Tourism and Social Assistance, Lefkoşa c/o Mersin 10, Turkey.

Entry Requirements
Nationals of the EU, Australia, Canada, New Zealand, the USA and many other countries do not require visas. Non EU visitors are not allowed to take up any form of employment or do business: obtain the necessary details and documents prior to arrival from the Migration Department, Lefkosia, tel: (22) 303138, fax: (22) 449221. Passports must be valid for at least 3 months beyond the date of entry into Cyprus.

Visitors to the south are allowed to make 2 day trips into the north (see p. 101). Check current regulations before planning a trip. Those holidaying in the north are not permitted, under any circumstances, to travel to the south.

Customs
Regulations permit import duty free of no more than 250g tobacco, 0.75l wine, 1l spirits, 150ml perfume and other articles totalling CY£50.00 from non-EU destinations. Cypriots arriving from abroad arrive laden, and foreigners are not often stopped. Cameras, laptop computers, and the like – all clearly valuable – are not in practice a problem.
Cars: Visitors can obtain a permit at the port to import a vehicle for three months free of taxes or duty, and can get further extensions of up to 12 months from the main Customs Office in Lefkosia. After this a car can be kept only if full duty is paid and the vehicle was less than two years old on arrival. Check current regulations as they do change.

Health Requirements
No certificate of vaccination is required, and Cyprus is free of epidemic diseases: malaria, once a scourge, has been eradicated.

Getting There
By air: The main point of entry is Larnaka International Airport, tel: (24) 643000. Pafos is a busy (and basic) secondary airport, tel: (24) 422835. Most scheduled flights are shared between Cyprus Airways (in which BA holds a 49% stake) and British Airways. Cyprus Airways' main office is at 21 Alkeou St, Lefkosia, tel: (22) 443054, with branches in other towns. There are two northern airports: **Ercan**, 25km (16 miles) east of Lefkosa and **Gecitale**, 30km (19 miles) northeast of Famagusta, but few direct flights are made because of international refusal to recognize the north as a separate state. Flights are, in the main, from or via Turkey.
By sea: Regular ferries connect Lemesos with Rhodes, Crete (Iraklion) and the Greek mainland (Piraeus, about 48hrs travel time). Prices vary according to

season. Ferries from Ancona and Venice travel to Cyprus via Patras (mainland Greece); ferries from Bari and Brindisi go to Patras, whence transfer can be made by land to Piraeus for boats to Lemesos. Israel and Egypt are reached by ferry from Lemesos, Syria and Lebanon from Larnaca.

The main northern port is Famagusta, with boats travelling to Syria and Turkey (Mersin). From Keryneia there are ferries to southern Turkish ports and a hovercraft service runs from Taşucu (May–Oct). **By car:** The major ferries to Lemesos from Greece and Italy transport motor vehicles.

Getting Around

Buses: Long-distance buses run between major towns and cities, at half-hour intervals except on Sunday. Urban services run 05:30–19:00, occasionally longer in the tourist season. Small operators connect villages and other communities: 'lorry bus' services may leave early for towns and return at the end of the working day. **Taxis:** Service taxis, usually extended Mercedes accommodating 4–7 people, pick up by pre-arrangement at hotels and homes. They cost far less than private taxis, but do not cover airports. Rural taxis are available in hill villages and resorts. In towns taxi fares are metered (surcharge between 23:00 and 06:00 and for more than one piece of luggage over 13kg, 29 pounds). **Road:** To **hire** a car you must be over 21 years of age and hold a valid driver's licence

(an international licence is not required). The large rental agencies are represented in most towns, at airports or through hotel reception, or book a car in advance through your travel agent. No mileage restrictions are imposed and **cheap diesel** is an important consideration when wavering between car or four-wheel drive. **Always pay for the collision damage waiver**, just a few pounds on the basic rental and well worth it, otherwise you could be liable for the first few hundred pounds in the event of a collision. Hire rates are reasonable compared with elsewhere in Europe.

Cars drive on the left, but taxi drivers sometimes forget and in the heat of summer people can be reckless. In towns and cities the **speed limit** is 50kph (30mph), on country roads 60kph (39mph) and motorways 100kph (60mph). A **horn** sounded behind you (or as a car passes) is not aggressive, it means 'I am overtaking'. Sound your horn when approaching bends with poor visibility. All hired cars have red number plates and an extra 'Z' on the number – some resident drivers feel obliged to overtake any 'Z' car and if overtaken by a female visitor male honour is slighted. Take care and, if in any doubt, don't! Vehicles approaching from the right have right of way.

Hitch-hiking: This is not generally favoured as a method of travel as it is so hot and dusty in summer, though villagers are very obliging. For young Cypriot conscripts surviving

on a pittance of an allowance it is a way of life.

Organized Tours: All hotels which participate in the package holiday trade offer day and half-day trips run by local companies in air-conditioned coaches with hotel pick-up.

What to Pack

In summer, lightweight cotton T-shirts and shorts suffice most of the time. In the mountains, summer evenings can be cold – pack a pullover and trousers. Sunhats and sunglasses make sense during the day. In more up-market hotels you might want more elegant clothes for evenings, but leave the tuxedo at home. In winter some days might be shirt-sleeve weather while others call for a pullover and waterproofs.

Money Matters

The CY£ is strong and stable, but following accession to the EU in 2004 Cyprus is likely to be an adopter of the euro, the common currency of much of the EU as early as 2008. The CY£ is subdivided into 100 cents. Notes are available in denominations of 50 cents, CY£1, 5, 10 and 20, and coins in 1, 2, 5, 10, 20 and 50 cents. Officially you can take out no more than CY£50; coming into Cyprus sums above £500 should be declared (but few do). Travellers' cheques can be imported without limit. In both airports exchange is available for all flights. A low crime rate means that many people come to Cyprus with their national currency rather than travellers' cheques.

In the north the currency is the Turkish lira, with its accompanying inflation. Many hotels accept CY£ as a foreign currency. Banks have inconvenient opening hours and red tape, and the rate is better in exchange houses which change currencies without commission.

Credit and debit cards including Visa, Mastercard and other cards which are part of the Cirrus/Maestro network can be used to withdraw local currency from ATMs throughout Cyprus (though in the North ATMs are few and far between). Due to the high rate of Turkish lira inflation, visitors to the north should withdraw/exchange small amounts of currency at a time to avoid carrying large wads of notes and being stuck with virtually useless Turkish currency on departure.

American Express has offices in Lefkosia, Lemesos and Larnaka.

Many garages accept notes or cards.

Tipping: A 10% service charge is included in hotel and restaurant bills, so tipping is not obligatory but small change is welcomed by taxi drivers, porters, waiters, etc.

Accommodation

From June to early September most hotels are geared to the pre-booked **package trade** – look for last-minute bargains from your travel agent. The CTO provides free brochures, listing hotels, apartments and other accommodation. **Prices** are government-controlled

according to category and, by law, rates must be displayed in hotel rooms. Outside the main season and major holidays such as Easter, finding accommodation on spec poses few problems: CTO offices can help. Pensions are few and far between, except in the northwest (Polis).

English is spoken at reception in all hotels.

Camping is officially permitted only at licensed campsites, though a flexible attitude is adopted by locals and visitors alike. There are six sites, five of which are on the coast.

Youth hostels exist in all the main centres: Lefkosia, tel: (22) 444808, Lemesos, tel: (25) 363749, Larnaka, tel: (24) 621508, Pafos, tel: (26) 232588 and in two forest areas: Troödos, tel: (25) 421649, and at the forest station, Stavros tis Psokas, tel: (26) 722338. An International Youth Hostel card is needed.

In the North: A complete listing of pensions and hotels is given in the Northern Cyprus Tourist Information brochure. All hotels have Turkish management, whether or not they were Greek-owned before 1974. Those that have always been Turkish-Cypriot owned are the **Saray** and Sabray's **Orient** in Lefkoşa, the **Acapulco** and **Celebrity** in Keryneia and the **Altun Tabya** and **Kutup** in Famagusta. There is an official **campsite** about 3km (2 miles) west of Keryneia. **Note:** Little provision is made for disabled visitors, who should contact the CTO for further information.

Business Hours

Shops in tourist areas stay open late and all day Sun. Elsewhere, from May–Sep shopping hours are: 08:00–13:00 and 16:00–19:00; Oct–Apr: 08:00–13:00 and 14:30–17:30; closed Wed, Sat afternoons and all day Sun. Public service hours: 07:30–14:30 Mon–Fri.

Banks: 08:15–12:30 Mon–Fri; and 15:00–17:30 in the main tourist areas.

Time

Cyprus is 2 hours ahead of Greenwich Mean Time, 1 hour ahead of Central European Time, and 7 hours ahead of US Eastern Standard Winter Time. Clocks go forward 1 hour on the last weekend in March, and back on the last Sunday in September.

Communications

Post: There are post offices in all towns, with poste-restante facilities in the main offices. Postage stamps are also sold by newsagents. Letters sent to the **north** of Cyprus have to go via Turkey – the code '**Mersin 10, Turkey**' must be added to the last line of the address.

Telephone: Cyprus is connected to 184 countries by direct dialling. **Directory enquiries**: dial 192 for local calls, and 194 for international calls. Cardphones and public payphones are widespread in all towns and villages, with dialling instructions in English and other languages.

Telecards (CY£2, 5 or 10) can be purchased from banks, post offices, souvenir shops and kiosks. Off-peak reduced rates operate for trunk calls between 20:00 and 07:00 and for international calls between 22:00 and 08:00 every day and all day Sun. Public **fax** is not available, but virtually all hotels will send and receive faxes for residents.

Electricity

The mains is 240 volts AC, supplied at 50Hz. Plugs are standard square-pin or two-pin continental: adaptors are widely available in supermarkets and most other stores. Batteries (including alkaline and Ni-Cad) are manufactured locally or imported and are available in all popular sizes in stores and garages.

Weights and Measures

The metric system has been used in the south since 1987, but some old Ottoman measures are still encountered: for weight the *oke* (~1.3kg or 2.8lb) and for land area the *dönüm* (~1350m^2 or 0.33 acres). In the north, the mile is used for distances.

Health Precautions

Walkers, naturalists and other explorers should make sure

that their **tetanus** protection is up to date.

It is easy to underestimate the strength of the **sun** – even short exposure on sensitive skins can leave a child or adult in agony. Use sun-hats, high-protection sun cream (renewed after swimming) and practise sensible sunbathing.

In the south Cypriots are fanatical about health: fruit and vegetables are scrupulously washed and food and water supplies are monitored by a strict public health inspectorate.

Condoms are readily available in pharmacies (Greek *profilaktika*; Turkish *preservatif*). **Natural hazards: Scorpions** are rare; large **millipedes** which sting are common, so check shoes and sleeping bags before use. The only truly venomous **snake** is the viper (*kufi*), for which anti-serum is available locally; the large black Montpellier snakes are harmless to humans. At the seaside, **weever fish** lie beneath the sand in shallow water with poisonous spines protruding. If you stand on one the pain is excruciating: put your foot in very hot water as quickly as

possible and get medical attention. Colourful **ragworms** (black, white and red) sting when touched anywhere on their bodies. **Sea urchins** are a painful nuisance but they are not poisonous – wear flip-flops.

Medical Services

Medical care in Cyprus is available through government-run general hospitals or private clinics. In emergencies, all the general hospitals have **casualty departments** and provide treatment free of charge, but you should make sure your **travel insurance** policy covers any other eventualities. English is almost inevitably spoken extremely well since many Cypriot doctors will have trained in the UK, USA or Canada. Consulting hours for private doctors are 09:00–13:00 and 16:00–19:00 on weekdays. **Pharmacies** stock all branded medicines, many of which are available without prescription. Those pharmacies open late at night and on weekends and holidays are listed in the newspapers.

Security

Cyprus is relatively crime-free. Until recently, **theft** from cars was unknown outside the Sovereign bases and most vehicles were left unlocked, but the incidence of theft from both cars and hotels has increased. The **police** are quite helpful and in villages they are very much part of local life. English is widely spoken so be polite if caught in a radar trap: your insults will be understood.

CONVERSION CHART		
FROM	**TO**	**MULTIPLY BY**
Millimetres	Inches	0.0394
Metres	Yards	1.0936
Metres	Feet	3.281
Kilometres	Miles	0.6214
Hectares	Acres	2.471
Litres	Pints	1.760
Kilograms	Pounds	2.205
Tonnes	Tons	0.984
To convert Celsius to Fahrenheit: x 9 ÷ 5 + 32		

Travel insurance is generally available as part of a package, or pre-booked separately through your travel agent.

Emergencies

Dial **199** for emergency services (ambulance, fire service, police). All-night pharmacies: dial **192**. In the north dial **155** for police, **112** for ambulance/paramedics, **177** for fire.

Etiquette

In monasteries and mosques visitors are expected to dress respectfully: no shorts or bare tops for men; women should cover bare arms or legs so as not to cause offence or be offended when admission to a place of worship is refused.

Language

In the south English is so widely spoken that it can be hard to practise your Greek (although people will be very pleased if you try). In hotels, shops and restaurants Cypriots have more than a smattering of German, French, Italian and even Arabic. In the north, many of the older Turkish Cypriots will speak English, but a few words of Turkish may prove very helpful and will be appreciated.

Photography

There is no shortage of subjects in Cyprus for the landscape, architectural or wildlife photographer. As elsewhere in the Mediterranean, the light is of better quality in spring and autumn. In general, avoid taking photographs in the hours around midday. In the morning and evening the longer shadows give better modelling and the slightly yellow light makes pictures warmer. Print film for your holiday snaps can be developed locally – there are outlets in all towns. Film deteriorates quickly in the heat (especially transparency), so serious photographers should bring their film with them to Cyprus. Buy film only where you know there will be a quick turnover. Photography is forbidden near any military area.

Good Reading

Davies, P. & J. and Huxley, A. (1983) *Wild Orchids of Britain and Europe*. Chatto & Windus, London.

Georgiades, Christos Ch. (1989) *Nature of Cyprus*. Lefkosia.

Jonsson, Lars (1992) *Birds of Europe with North Africa and the Middle East*. Helm, London.

Karageorghis, Vassos (1982) *Cyprus from the Stone Age to the Romans*. Thames & Hudson, London.

Oberling, Pierre (1983) *The Road to Bellapais: The Turkish Cypriot Exodus to Northern Cyprus*. Columbia UP, USA.

Pantelas et al (1993) *Cyprus Flora in Colour – The Endemics*. Lefkosia.

Panteli, Stavros, History of Modern Cyprus (2005), Interworld Publications.

USEFUL PHRASES		
ENGLISH	**GREEK**	**TURKISH**
yes	*né*	*evet*
no	*ókhi*	*hayir*
hello	*khérete*	*merhaba*
how are you?	*ti kánete?*	*nasılsınız?*
goodbye	*adio*	*allahaısmarladık*
please	*parakaló*	*lütfen*
thank you	*efkharistó*	*teşekkür ederim*
sorry/excuse me	*signómi*	*affedersiniz*
how much is?	*póso iné?*	*kaç para?*
when?	*poté?*	*né zaman?*
where?	*pou?*	*nerede?*
I'd like	*thélo*	*istiyorum*
open	*aniktó*	*açik*
closed	*kleistó*	*kapalı*
one	*éna*	*bir*
two	*dhío*	*iki*
three	*tría*	*üç*
four	*téssera*	*dört*
five	*pénte*	*beş*
six	*éxi*	*altı*
seven	*eftá*	*yedi*
eight	*okhtó*	*sekiz*
nine	*enniá*	*dokuz*
ten	*dhéka*	*on*

INDEX

Page numbers in **bold**
indicate illustrations.